Lemonade Stand Economics

Geof White

For information regarding reproduction, contact info@LemonadeStandEconomics.com

For information about special discounts for bulk purchases or speaking engagements by the author, please contact
info@LemonadeStandEconomics.com

Cover art design created by design workshop students Carliann Holso, Bruce Purdy, and Curt Trepanier of Appleton Career Academy, 2012. © Geof White 2012

Additional designs shown in "The Story Behind the Cover" created by the following Appleton Career Academy workshop students: Megan Bast, Kate Burmeister, Ben Collar, Carliann Holso, Laura Larabell, Nikki Preradovic, Bruce Purdy, Soniya Regmi, Mackenzie Schmitt, and Curt Trepanier, 2012.

ISBN-10: 0985811234
EAN-13: 9780985811235

To my sons, Jack and Sam, who mean the world to me

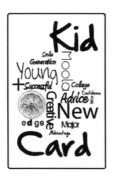

ACKNOWLEDGMENTS

Writing a book is a big project that no person can do alone. Many people helped create *Lemonade Stand Economics*.

Kim Graff, my editor and book shepherd – You coached, guided, encouraged, researched, edited, proofread, and turned someone who had never written anything into a published author. You believed in *Lemonade Stand Economics* from day one, and for that I am forever grateful. There is no one I would rather work with …and you are the reason this book will help students.

Robert J. Felton, book designer/illustrator – First, thank you for being Robert. Your view of life is inspiring, and your illustrative genius is as important to *Lemonade Stand Economics* as the writing. You are also the ideal example of how to work for yourself, have fun, and pay your own way…for which I have the absolute highest respect.

Renee Ulman and the staff of Appleton Career Academy – Thank you for supporting the vision of *Lemonade Stand Economics* and providing us valuable classroom time to present our material.

Thanks to the students at ACA. Your involvement has been invaluable. Bruce, Curt, and Carli, thank you for taking your design class seriously and creating the best damn book cover around! Mackenzie, thank you for exceeding all expectations and creating my favorite tie ever! Soniya, thank you for bringing your marketing skills and drive to LSE. Dan—*Dan the Video Man*—thank you for your videography talents as well as oversleeping that one morning, which gave us the lemon-juggling concept.

Thanks to the students who are featured on the LSE website and video testimonials: Chloe, Cerise, Dalton, Tallyn, Lindsay, Taylor, Steph, and Jordan. Sarah, Marc, Robert, Jason, Mackenzie, Soniya, Bryanna, and Jesse.

Mia and our initial focus group – Thank you for hating the original book title. Thank you for telling us what students want to read. Your honesty steered us in the right direction.

All of the test readers and proofreaders – Thank you for crossing out, starring, and smiley facing the initial manuscript. Your input was invaluable in the writing of this book.

RJ Foster, the wordsmith – Thank you for articulately squeezing the most out of our sweet idea and eloquently expressing the book's concept in its most important three words: the title.

David Jon Finch – Thank you for dropping everything and helping us with graphics when we needed it most.

Adam Bordeaux – Thank you for your writing skills in the beginning and your video editing skills after completion.

Thank you to the Allman Brothers Band and Jimi Hendrix, as most of *Lemonade Stand Economics* was written listening to your fine music.

Valley Window Cleaning – Thank you to the VWC team for doing a fantastic job keeping the business running smoothly and being the best structural transparency and plane surface cosmological engineers around.

Connie Gisel – Thank you for being my favorite window cleaning customer.

Marc and Steve Wasserman and Rochester Window Cleaning – Thank you for taking a fifteen-year-old kid and turning him into the best damn window cleaner around.

Jack Genthner – Thank you for being a mentor in my high school years, even though I was too young to realize what you were doing.

My mom, Nancy Verlinde – Thank you for raising me to be what I am today and especially for always encouraging my early entrepreneurial endeavors, which made this book possible.

My sister, Natalie Goran – Thank you for always supporting me and making sure I know that I am your favorite putz.

My family: Jen, Jack, Sam, and Jason – More than anyone, you have seen the ups and downs of writing this book. Thank you for your patience and for believing in me. I never could have written this masterpiece without your support.

All my other friends and family – Thanks for asking about the book, listening when I talked about it, and supporting me. You know who you are…I won't forget you.

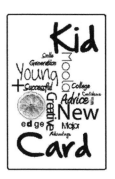

CONTENTS

THERE IS A STORY BEHIND
THE COVER OF THIS BOOK...

Or I should say there is a story behind the amazing high school students who created it.

We've all heard the saying, "You can't judge a book by its cover." Well, this is especially true if you've written a book and don't have a cover. People are visual and the cover design is critical in the success of any book. During our research we saw this many, many times while looking at competing titles. Much of the content was good—even great—but the books didn't sell well because of the cover. Maybe the covers were off-putting, didn't convey the content correctly, or targeted the wrong audience. The content in this book will help many high school students, but only if they read it.

I'm a lot of things: a business owner, an entrepreneur, a husband and father, an author. But I am not a graphic designer. I know what I like, and I know what is most likely to resonate with customers. But I am not a designer. However, I do know designers, so I did the logical thing and contacted them.

I met with freelancers, advertising agencies, and graphic design firms to explain the content and vision of the book. I actually gave some of the designers early drafts of the manuscript to aid in the creative process. It was a long road and, quite frankly, expensive and frustrating. Nobody got it. I looked at the graphics and concepts the professionals had produced, and not one of them was even close to the eye-catching and thought provoking cover in my head. So I put the cover on the back burner and moved forward with focus groups and further developing the manuscript and its content.

And that is where the story behind the cover really began. Exactly like I wrote in the book, the cover was all about networking, relationships, and the extending and accepting of opportunities. I was looking for a book cover, but I discovered so much more.

I had been writing for more than a year, and there was no book cover. In one of the weekly book meetings with my editor, I said "Hey, we need a kid to design the cover! After all, the book is written for high school students; but where can we find a kid who can design a book cover? There are no ads on Craigslist that say, "High School Student Looking to Design Book Covers."

So my editor and I started where we were. We asked the student who had helped set up the focus groups for us, who happened to be an art student, if she was interested. We thought she'd say, "Yeah, I'd like to design a book cover." But she is a *fine art* student—sculpture, paintings, and the like—so she wasn't right for this type of art. However, she knew someone who might be able to help and referred us.

On this student's referral, we approached the Appleton Career Academy (ACA), which is a charter school inside a large local high school. ACA is a different school, and when I say different I mean *way* different. The teachers teach differently and the students learn in a different way.

The program is very project-based, career-focused, and performance-driven. We met with ACA's director and immediately saw that she understood the concept behind *Lemonade Stand Economics* and our search for a book cover. We offered an opportunity for her students to participate, and she accepted. She was gracious, helpful, confident, and approachable. We knew we had a good fit.

27 students + 35 days + 1 book cover = 1 big opportunity

We felt good but realized this was a huge risk. I had promised a class of high school design students that the best cover in the class was going to be the face of my book. To state the importance of a book cover is not easy, so there was a risk. Now back to that opportunity...

On the first day of the five-week workshop, my editor and I addressed the class. We discussed how opportunity is a two-way street. Someone has to extend an opportunity and someone has to accept that opportunity. We were there to extend an opportunity: *So here it is, kids. We need the best possible book cover, so let's get to work.* In response we got a couple good questions and a few blank stares. Later my editor and I said to each other, "Please, just let us have one or two good covers to choose from."

Ten days later we went back to ACA and met with the students to get a look at their initial designs and be sure they were even close to barking up the right tree. We answered their questions and offered advice, suggestions, and any direction we could think of that would help produce the best damn book cover around. The initial designs were really good, better than what we had expected.

Among the students was a young lady by the name of Mackenzie. When she sat down, she introduced herself politely and then confidently laid her book cover design before us. I looked at her design, and any worries I had felt about the riskiness of this endeavor flew out the window. After about five seconds, I looked at my editor, raised my eyebrows, turned to Mackenzie and said, "I wouldn't change a thing." Her design was amazing. Better than anything we could have imagined. But what was *amazing* didn't end there. Not by a long shot. There were several cover designs that were amazing. These students blew us away.

Initially when we thought of having a student design the cover, we were hoping for two good covers to choose from. But that's not what happened. There were too many good ones to choose from—one great design after another. All unique, professional, great designs. What we found truly incredible was that the students all had the same material to work with: a book title, a subtitle, and the author's name. Yet all the covers looked completely different. These students had put their personalities into the project.

We had celebrity judges (local business people, the mayor) come in and vote for their favorites. We had people vote through a Facebook contest, which turned into an unforeseen teaching opportunity.

These students went out and lobbied for their covers. They handed out cards that said *vote for me*, they mass-texted, and one student had her cousin announce the contest on a Texas radio station. Two other students announced via Facebook that they would dye their hair blue and purple if they won. Oh, and we can't forget one student's mom. She dominated the Facebook marketing campaign for team 14.

The contest was a lot of work, but it was also a lot of fun and incredibly energizing and educational. You could feel the electricity in the air. These students came up with amazing designs, worked hard and smart at marketing their covers, and left us with a decision to make.

The illustrator, editor, and I met after the contest was over to tally everything up. It was unanimous but not easy. Obviously, if you are reading this book, you have seen the design, which was exactly the book cover we were looking for. So thank you, Bruce, Curt, and Carli!

Yes, I got a great book cover out of this experience, but that was not the best part. The designs were beyond impressive, and so were the students. They took the opportunity seriously. They worked hard. They were excited and got other people excited, too. After we had our winner, we decided to give credit to some of the other designs.

Any of the designs you see here could have been on the cover. Please take a look at them so you can understand how impressive those ACA students are. You never know...maybe a couple of these designs will appear on future books.

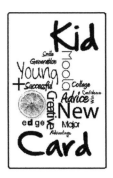

INTRODUCTION

Lemonade Stand Economics:
A refreshing way to pay for college

When you are seven years old, having a lemonade stand is a fun way to spend the afternoon. You stir up some lemonade mix with your mom, create a cool sign with crayons and a piece of cardboard, and stand out on the corner waiting for passersby to stop and give you quarters while you overfill plastic cups with lemonade. Simple enough: sell a few cups of delicious lemonade and earn a few quarters. Provide a tasty product to a thirsty paying consumer.

Although you may not realize it when you are seven, there is much more to that childhood lemonade stand than just handing out lemonade for quarters. The lemonade stand is the most fundamental and understandable model for business. Let's start with the lemonade itself. Mom makes the lemonade unless you make it yourself, but my guess is that Mom's lemonade tastes much better than yours. Mom also paid for the lemonade as well as the cups and everything you needed to make the crayon sign that says, "Lemonade 25 Cents."

All of that is called overhead, and every business has it. Overhead, or expenses, is the term for all the items you need to be able to provide that cup of lemonade to your customer. It's a good investment for your mom. She figures it's worth the $2.59 she paid for cups because she knows where you are and that you are out of her hair for a few hours doing something safe and productive.

When did you set up your lemonade stand? Did you do it at 8:00 a.m. when the sun is coming up and people are eating breakfast or 8:00 p.m. when it's getting dark and the mosquitoes are out? Did you set it up if it was raining or cold? Of course not. You set it up on a sunny afternoon. You need to provide the product people want when they are most likely to buy it. People don't necessarily say, "Wow, I'm thirsty and hot. I wish I had a tall, cool glass of lemonade right now." But your lemonade stand has the big *Lemonade 25 Cents* sign. You are now advertising by power of suggestion. You are informing potential customers that you can help quench that afternoon thirst.

You set up your lemonade stand where people can see it. Maybe you write "Ice Cold" before the word lemonade on your sign. Maybe you put a couple balloons on the stand to get people's attention. You make sure the *25 Cents* is in big letters so people know that for only a quarter they get a refreshing cup of lemonade.

When a customer does walk up to the lemonade stand, how do you greet that person? Do you say hi? Do you say, "Can I get you some lemonade?" These are the basics of customer service. Are we really using the term customer service with a seven-year-old's lemonade stand? Yes, except the level of expectation regarding customer service from a child is pretty low. Nobody expects a kid to provide excellent customer service, but that changes as you get older and start charging more than a quarter for something.

What happens if that seven-year-old has a lemonade stand for a couple hours three days a week in a busy neighborhood all summer? Maybe he or she makes a few bucks each day. Saving up for that bike is much easier because those bucks add up over time—especially if Mom keeps buying the cups and lemonade. One person provides the labor and nets the profit while the other pays all of the overhead. The next thing you know, after a few weeks all the neighbors are talking about the kid who has the lemonade stand down the street. Adults love the hard-working kid and will go out of their way to help by buying a cup or two.

This book is not written for the seven-year-old manning a lemonade stand. This book is for high school students who need to make some money to pay for college...using the lessons and principles that began at a childhood lemonade stand.

I started cleaning windows for myself when I was seventeen. When I graduated from college at age twenty-three, I was still working for myself cleaning windows; but I was more efficient, more knowledgeable, and making significantly more money. My cups of lemonade were clean windows and I collected dollar bills, not quarters.

If you woke me up in the middle of the night from a dead sleep and asked me, "Where did you learn most of your business skills?" I would say, "When I cleaned windows as a teenager." The skills you learn while working for yourself in high school—work ethic, money management, time management, and customer service—are the foundation you will need during your adult career. When I learned to deal with customers at the age of seventeen, I had no idea that, once I graduated from college, those skills would be the most important business skills carried forward into adulthood. Everything I learned in college courses—well, most of it—was important, but I would never have been successful without those basic skills learned as a teenager working for myself.

I provided the best possible service a teenager could, and I charged for it. Eventually I was charging $50 an hour, and my summer days were booked solid. Back then I thought cleaning windows was a great way to pay for college—because it was. Now I look back and realize that making $50 an hour wasn't nearly as impressive as the business skills I learned on my entrepreneurial journey. I worked extremely hard and discovered that customers will pay a premium if the value matches that premium price. The better the lemonade tastes, the more quarters in your pocket. Customers will pay a premium for the best damn lemonade in town. That's how I paid for college and that's why my business is successful now—because of the foundation of sound business practices I learned as a teenager.

So why is it important that I help teenagers work for themselves and pay their own way through college? Because the world doesn't need another college graduate with huge student loans. Did you know that only 5 % of college students work for themselves? The other 95 % work low-paying jobs where the boss tells them when and how to work and then cuts a small paycheck at the end of the week. On top of that, these kids are taking out enormous student loans and thus saddled with years of debt after graduation. Congratulations! You graduated from college. Now here's a bill for $20,000 or $50,000 or $150,000!

With a little hard work and forethought, students can graduate with no debt. So why don't more students do that? Simple. Because most students don't know that it's even possible. Most don't know where to start. I did it, and Lemonade Stand Economics can steer you in the right direction so you can, too. It's easier than you think. If you had a lemonade stand when you were a kid, then you've already got the basics down.

As a business owner, I get hit up by everyone I know—and everyone they know —who has a teenager looking for a summer job. These kids are willing to work for me for $10 an hour. And that's great! I am all about a teenager who's willing to work, and I can almost always use another hardworking crew member. On the other hand, I have never had a kid put a flyer on my door that says, "I need to pay for college and I will clean your windows." Or mow your lawn, or paint some rooms, or rake your leaves, or tutor your kids. All of which will pay more than double that $10 an hour—and all of which I need to have done. This kid wouldn't even have to sell me on the idea. He'd just have to say, "Hey, I can do this for you." and the deal would be done. But to this day, no teenager has *asked* for my business yet.

So where are these students, the statistical 5 % who are working for themselves? The ones who earn two or three times what their peers make. Where are the teens who educate themselves in business skills every summer? All I can do is wonder why no one seems to be doing what I did. There is a market for teens who want to work for themselves and get paid for it. Maybe *you* are one of them.

Working for yourself. . . "That's a lot of work." I hear this all the time. "I'll just get a job; it's easier and they will guarantee me forty hours a week." I get that. You will get your forty hours. It's easier. You show up, punch in, do as much work as you have to, and then punch out and go home. Most of the American workforce does that. So you will make your $8 an hour no matter how hard you work—or how hard you don't. You might make eight sandwiches a day or 80 sandwiches. Either way after eight hours you will make $64. But what if you did things differently? What if there was a way to find your own customers and make $300 or $400 in that same eight hours? Would you do it? Is it worth the extra effort?

You want easy? Put down this book.
You want to work smart and make more money? Keep reading.

When I started working for myself in high school, I never ran out of jobs. Jobs are everywhere. You just need to find them. It takes effort, and most people don't want to exert the effort required to find customers. It's that simple. Most people get a job and receive a paycheck at the end of the week because it's simple...it's traditional...it's normal. Most people are employees, and there is nothing wrong with that. Roads need to be built, papers need to be filed and coffee needs to be served. The world needs employees. Heck, I need employees. I've been an employee a few times myself. Apply for the job, get the job, show up to do the job, and receive a paycheck. But I would much rather make money for myself instead of making money for someone else. I call it entrepreneurial spirit and I'm glad I have it. Maybe you have it, too.

Ask yourself these questions:
- Are you always the person who questions everything?
- Did you ever think, "I wonder what would happen if we did it *my* way?"
- Do you say, "I can do it better than that guy!"
- Do you imagine what other people will say when you are successful?

- Are you willing to take on the responsibility of creating your own opportunities?
- Are you disciplined enough to work your own hours and schedule your own work?
- Would you rather make money for yourself with your knowledge and skill?

If you answered yes to any of the above questions you may just have some entrepreneurial spirit in you. If none of these remind you of yourself, then working for yourself is probably not for you. There is no right or wrong; it's a matter of personal choice. I very much prefer to make my own opportunities, work my own hours, choose the work I do, and keep all the profit for myself. If you think you might, too, harness your entrepreneurial spirit and use your own unique ideas to create opportunities. Utilize your skills, make wise decisions, and squeeze the lemons you were handed. Learn from your mistakes, but keep going. Don't make excuses, just get to work!

When I drive around neighborhoods doing estimates, I never pass a kid's lemonade stand without stopping. Never. I always stop. There is a particular stand that I remember. It's run by a girl maybe nine or ten years old in a suburb where I often work. I have bought lemonade from her five or six times. Not only does she offer lemonade but red Kool-Aid and cookies, too. She has an upsell product: chocolate chip cookies with purple sprinkles. She sells cookies with some lemonade to wash them down—brilliant! She is very polite, and I don't pay her in quarters. I pay her in dollar bills. I know she is out there a lot of the time, so whenever I'm in that neighborhood I drive by her corner to see if she's selling her cookies and lemonade that day. I am a repeat customer. Now the fact that I am paying her a little extra for a few glasses of lemonade isn't going to turn that kid into the next Fortune 500 CEO. But, for a split second, I hope she looks down in her hand and thinks, "Wow, I made this much just by selling lemonade? This is awesome!"

I didn't sell lemonade for quarters. I cleaned windows. I was the best damn window cleaner in town, and I charged accordingly. This book is about learning to charge more than a quarter, to provide a level of service that people will pay top dollar for. You need to charge enough to pay for that college degree. Go ahead and flip your middle finger at the college student loan department. You don't need them. You are smarter and harder-working than that. You aren't selling lemonade now because a quarter isn't enough. You aren't saving for a new bike; you are saving for a college degree—an investment in yourself. Costs are higher and so are expectations, yet the system to pay for that college education is as simple as your neighborhood lemonade stand.

The goal here is to show you how you can make the most dollars per hour doing what *you* want to do, something you enjoy or have an interest in. I did it. I cleaned windows charging $50 an hour as a teenager. On a good day, I made $400. On a bad day, maybe $100. If I were a sandwich artist making $8 an hour, it would take fifty hours to make $400. But I made that much in a single day. One day vs. six days.

Lemonade Stand Economics is simple math that makes a big difference. Whether you want to just pay for college or begin a long-term business empire, read on. I'm going to throw a boatload of information at you. Use what you need, remember as much as you can, refer back when you have to…but get to work. There's a lot to do.

We'll work quickly and efficiently, setting goals, marketing, bidding jobs, and serving up a steamin' hot plate of fantastic customer service. Once in this money making rhythm you will make enough to pay for college, graduate with no debt and maybe even have a few bucks left over in your bank account. Let your little brother run the lemonade stand now, it's time to make some real money.

CHAPTER 1

Lemonade or financial aid? It's your choice

Don't sign anything until you finish this book

You cracked this book because you don't know how you are going to pay for your college education. Your parents are in no position to pay for it, and your part-time job barely covers gas money. This leaves you with two options: pay for college as you go with money that you earn or take out student loans and pay for it later.

No one needs to preach to you about the benefits of going to college, yet no one is telling you how to pay for it either. It's up to you. Are you going to simply take the loan that is handed to you? Fill out the student loan form, sign the personal guarantee to pay it back after graduation, and go to class? That's what 90 % of the people reading this will do. Or are you part of that smart, bold, creative 10 % that is willing to work hard *now* to make things easier in the future? And when I say easier in the future, I mean much easier—relieving yourself from years of debt. Working for yourself now and earning more money than the next guy is significantly less stressful than being a slave to debt for years after graduation.

Many of you are reading this because someone told you to. You will skim it and toss it aside and never think of it again. However, if you are looking for some real help with your financial future, this book could change your life. The world consists of motivated leaders and perhaps not-so-motivated followers. If I had to put numbers on it, I would say 10 % are motivated leaders and 90 % are followers. The leaders are more confident and harder-working. They create their own destiny as well as creating the destiny of the followers.

Yes, leaders are motivated. I call it *being the 10*. Look at the motivation spectrum below. Are you the teenager who is highly motivated (a 10) or are you completely unmotivated (a 1)? Or are you somewhere in between? There is no right or wrong, and you can always move yourself within the spectrum. If you consider yourself a 10 on the motivational spectrum then you are already one huge step ahead of the rest. Which one are you? Do you have the attitude, confidence, motivation, and—in the same breath—the humility to be the 10?

Motivation Spectrum

Fast-forward in your mind to your college graduation. You are standing there in your cap and gown, and someone hands you a well-deserved diploma that you earned after four years of hard work. What a joyous day! You graduated. Your parents are so proud! You are now ready to start adulthood with a college degree in your back pocket. But wait! Remember back in high school, when you wondered how you were going to pay for this education, and you signed on the dotted line? Then each and every semester you signed again…right below where it says, "payments commence upon graduation." Buzzkill! Attached to that diploma is a bill—a big bill. You owe $20,000, or maybe it's $50,000 or maybe $150,000. Whatever that total is, it will take you years to pay it off as the interest clock ticks.

Fast-forward even farther—ten or twenty years more—and you are still making a monthly payment on that student loan. Why? Because waaaaaay back in high school you decided to take what seemed like the easy road and sign on the dotted line. So back to that crucial moment in high school—*right now!*—you have two options.

Option One – Pay for school as you go and graduate debt-free. It's much less painful for a shorter time frame and will increase your business knowledge exponentially year to year.

Option Two – Take out student loans and pay them back after graduation. It's easier now but will cause financial stress for years after graduation and cost you more over time due to interest. Additionally you will learn your business lessons later in life while making money for someone else.

According to the National Postsecondary Student Aid Study conducted by the US Department of Education, updated in January 2010, 67% of students graduating from four-year colleges and universities had student loan debt. This is an increase of 27% from 2004.

My story

In seventh grade I was suspended from school for selling firecrackers to other students. Now, as a father of two young boys, I realize what a huge mistake that was. Fireworks are dangerous, and selling them to friends at school was wrong. What thirteen-year-old Geof would do is find an older kid to buy a brick of firecrackers for about $20, then turn around and sell them to all his friends by the pack for $1 apiece. A brick came with eighty packs of firecrackers, which means on each $20 brick I made a $60 profit. What did I do with that extra $60? I spent some of it on football cards, candy, video games, and the like; but I always spent a portion on buying more firecrackers. At the time I didn't know what profit was. I was just having fun and making some cash doing it. But I did learn from the experience that if I spent $20 and added a little sales effort, I could make $80. That effort was worth $60. This was one of my earliest lessons in turning a profit.

It wasn't long before I got caught and suspended from school. This was an in-school suspension, meaning I got to spend the day in the principal's office. My mother had to come to school and *discuss* the incident with the principal. Needless to say, my mother was not happy. So what did I learn from this experience? Selling firecrackers wasn't a good idea, especially at school. It's illegal and dangerous. However, on a positive note, I learned that with a little extra effort you can make money off practically anything. While business opportunities are almost everywhere, some opportunities are smart and others are just plain dumb. I put selling firecrackers at school in the dumb category. Mowing the neighbor's lawn for $25? I would put that in the smart category.

I was a typical kid. I played video games, fooled around playing football, ate snacks, drank soda, and rode my bike. I saw my mother head off to work every morning, and many times she would come home and go back to another job that same night. That's why being summoned to the principal's office to discuss the firecracker incident was even worse. She had to ask her boss for the morning off to deal with her son's escapade. You see, my mother was the stereotypical single working mom with two kids. She could afford food, rent, clothing, Christmas presents, and school tuition but not much more. She worked long hours at two jobs, sometimes three.

Many people would assume I saw this and said to myself, "I'm never going to live that way." But it wasn't like that. What I learned was that it's okay to work hard, to give your best regardless of what you are doing. My mom believed that. She did secretarial work every day and waited tables many nights. She worked hard and did what she had to do to pay the bills. She had a good work ethic, and my work ethic is a direct result of hers. The difference between us was the money. She made less than $15 per hour. At the same time as a teenager, I was charging upwards of $40 or $50 per hour. *An hour of work is an hour of work. If you work hard, make sure you are charging enough for your time.* [Sweet Tip]

I'm not certain exactly when I started down the entrepreneurial path, but I've always had an attraction to business. Over the years, working for myself brought successes and failures. I want to share these life lessons with you so you can minimize the failures and increase the successes in your own entrepreneurial endeavors. And don't let the term *entrepreneurial endeavors* scare you.

Being an entrepreneur simply means that you are working for yourself and charging people for doing what you choose to do. You are an individual with unique thoughts, ideas, and skills. The entrepreneur uses those unique skills to make money. You are your own boss playing by your own rules. When I was thirteen posting flyers for yard-work jobs, I was just looking to make some money to buy a bike. I did not realize that in reality I was introducing myself to the world as an entrepreneur.

I held many low-paying jobs when I was young, running the gamut of what most kids do for their first jobs. I babysat, mowed and raked lawns, shoveled snow, delivered newspapers, and worked at a gas station, grocery store, and hardware store...you name it, I did it. I needed spending money, so I worked. Then I got a summer job in high school cleaning windows, and everything changed. You see, I did something the next summer, when I was seventeen, that changed my brain. I started cleaning windows for myself. I found the customers, I performed the work, and I kept the profit. I was making money for myself rather than making money for someone else. My specialty was cleaning windows, but I was also happy to do any other side job the customer needed done as well. I cleaned out garages, painted, cleaned gutters, trimmed bushes—whatever my customers would pay me to do. I needed spending cash and I needed to pay for college.

I'll be using my own personal experience as a window cleaner throughout this book. By the end you'll either never want to read the words *window cleaner* and *squeegee* again, or you'll be one and own several. What I did took ambition, creativity, and a lot of hard work, but it was also fun. Yes, I said *fun*! And I met some fantastic people along the way.

Keep in mind that all the hard work you'll do is for *yourself*. You're not putting money in someone else's pocket anymore, just your own. I make no promises that this will be easy. In fact, I guarantee it won't be easy. Working for yourself is just that: work. But the financial and educational reward is much greater than you'll receive from that low-paying job. Isn't it worth the extra effort to make twice as much money working for yourself??

In many ways you'll be learning from two different schools simultaneously during this period. You'll learn important business skills while working for yourself, at the same time gaining academic knowledge through your high school curriculum. You'll be doubling your skill set and will have twice as much to put on your resume when you graduate from college.

Whether you decide to work for someone else or continue on an entrepreneurial journey, the skills you learn now will be valuable, marketable, and real in the future. Plan as we might, none of us knows where our career path will take us or when it will take us there. Never in a million years would I have guessed on that first day I picked up a squeegee as a sophomore in high school that I would own and operate a large window cleaning business twenty-five years later...or be writing a book helping others realize how rewarding working for yourself can be.

Statistics say that the average college graduate will change jobs every five years. So if you work forty years from ages twenty-five through sixty-five, you'll change jobs at least eight times. From my own experience, I'll tell you that it's not just employers you'll change but job duties and responsibilities as well. To navigate this successfully, you need transferable skills that can be applied to various industries. This is what working for yourself will provide. Customer service skills, time management, marketing, advertising, selling, and dealing with expenses and revenue are all real skills. They are interwoven into every profession in some way, shape, or form. The earlier you learn these skills, the farther you will be ahead of your peers and the more prepared you will be not only for your first job out of college but for life.

My training

The day I picked up that first squeegee at age sixteen was the day that set me on a path to successfully putting myself through college on my own dime. I didn't know it at the time, but I was getting a valuable education during that summer job. I learned to clean windows working for Rochester Window Cleaning (RWC) in Rochester, New York. The owners, Mark and Steve Wasserman, took me under their wing and taught me the tricks of the trade. All the other employees were seasoned professionals, and this was key in creating the proper mindset and skill training for me to go out on my own. *There is no better way to learn a trade or skill than to work alongside professionals.* {**Sweet Tip**} I can't stress this point enough. To successfully make more money working for yourself, you must be willing to focus on learning rather than earning for three to six months. Go into that summer job knowing you're trying to learn as much as possible in as little time as possible. That summer taught me a whole list of skills that I would call on later when I went to work for myself...at the ripe old age of seventeen.

RWC hired me as summer help and paid me $3.35 an hour. If I worked a full week, I would take home $114 after taxes...forty hours of work for $114. I was lucky. "Lucky to be making that amount of money?" you might ask. Well, sort of. At that time $3.35 was only minimum wage, but I was truly lucky because I was being paid to learn a trade. It was a top-notch education. I learned to clean commercial windows, residential windows, and high-rise windows. I learned how to deal with customers, how to walk ledges, proper ladder safety, and the list goes on. These guys were pros, and their professionalism couldn't help but rub off on me. Aside from all the technical aspects of window cleaning, I learned how attitude, a good work ethic, and creating a culture of fantastic customer service make the day run smoothly and create profits.

All of these skills came in handy when I started working for myself cleaning windows. In fact, they're all still valuable to this day. I did better in job interviews after college because of these qualities. I advanced my career because of these qualities. I lead employees better because of these qualities. How you conduct business is a direct result of your attitude, work ethic, and values—all of which the customer sees in your level of customer service. Again, all you have to do is add some effort to your skill; and those customers will start paying the profit that pays for your college education.

Work ethic, customer service, and playing the Kid Card

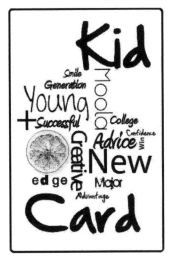

People have lots of ideas of what *work ethic* means. Certainly you've heard cranky old men saying, "You kids these days have no work ethic. You have it easy! Video games and cell phones all the time. That's all kids do." If you haven't heard this, just imagine an old man saying those words. Got the wrinkly old fellow pictured in your head? Good. Now back to the work ethic. A person with a good work ethic values and appreciates hard work. How you work is important and how you treat the idea of work is just as important. And when I say *hard work*, I don't mean lugging heavy bags of bricks uphill. In any job there is hard work. It may come in the form of tight deadlines or cleaning that one hard-to-reach skylight or getting the images set just right for a website. Farm kids have a reputation for having a great work ethic. Why? Because they were taught to value work from an early age. Farmers and their children are known for starting early, working long hours, and doing hard work on the farm every day.

Are you working as hard as you can? Are you getting your work done the right way and in an efficient manner? Or are you taking a lot of breaks, texting your friends, goofing off, and being lazy? When you have a good work ethic, it shows. Customers see it. Coworkers see it. Everyone sees it. Maybe you offer to stay late on the job to get it done. Maybe you have to work in less-than-desirable conditions, or you go to work when your friends want you to call in sick so you can join them at the beach for the day. Maybe you are pleasant and professional even when you are having a bad day or a customer is rude to you.

Customer service is the absolute most important part of working for yourself. If your customers are happy—meaning you did what was expected of you (and hopefully more)—then they will continue to hire you. Poor customer service almost always guarantees you will not have a repeat customer. Not only is the chance very likely your customer will not call you back, but it's also very likely he or she will tell others of the bad experience with you. Avoid poor customer service like you would the mystery meat in your school lunch. Avoid poor customer service like the proverbial plague. That is the great thing about working for yourself: it's in your control to avoid poor customer service. You can serve the best damn lemonade in town *and* provide the best customer service—it's completely up to you.

Customers have expectations; exceed them or fail. Customers are the lifeblood of any business; treat them well and you'll succeed. Treat them poorly, and you'll be working for someone else again before you know it.

Treating your customers well means treating them with respect and always being polite. I know, did this guy really just tell me to be polite and respectful? Yes, I did, because I see a lot of teenagers who aren't polite or respectful. And believe me, your customers will notice, too. Customers love the polite, hard-working high school student. Use that to your advantage: play the Kid Card.

Throughout this book you will see the term *play the Kid Card*. Sometimes there is an advantage to being seen as a kid. While referring to you as a *kid* is technically incorrect, it will happen. Obviously it would be more accurate to refer to you as a young adult. However, your customers will undoubtedly be older than you are; and anyone over the age of thirty often refers to a high school student as a kid. My advice is to get past the term and use it to your advantage. Yes, use the fact that you are a kid to these people as an advantage.

Most adults love the ambitious, hardworking kid who is working to pay for college. That appreciation is a huge advantage for you when it comes to working for yourself. Whether it helps you get more business, charge a higher rate, or bail yourself out when you make a mistake, use the fact that you are a kid to your benefit. Admit to being a kid when you need it, but always act like the young adult you are. So play the Kid Card, but don't abuse it. Just play it when it makes sense. It's a great foundation for great customer service.

I can't even count how many new customers I added to my contact list by having a good work ethic and providing excellent customer service to just one customer. If you impress one customer, then that one customer will tell his friends and neighbors what a good job you did and how professional you were as you solved his problems and exceeded his expectations. He might even mention how you thanked him and shook his hand after the job was done.

That old saying, "The customer is always right" has been around so long for a reason. My own version goes something like this: "Although the customer is not always right, treat him/her as though he/she is." Employ the words, *absolutely, sure thing*, and *not a problem* often, and of course use *please* and *thank you* all the time. *Customers may be leery of an inexperienced young man or woman doing work for them. Make the customer feel comfortable with you.* [**Sweet Tip**] Use words and actions and a positive, get-it-done attitude to reassure customers that you can and will exceed their expectations.

Customer service is a quickly disappearing aspect of American business. Take notice of how friendly (or not!) the clerk at your local sandwich shop is the next time you visit. It seems today most employees just don't care. They are tired or they hate their job or they didn't get the weekend off as requested. Even if those things are all true for you, don't be that person. Be the opposite. Be the positive go-getter that your grandparents want you to be. Chances are you'll set yourself apart and develop a spotless reputation if you just employ simple customer service skills.

Customer service skills are best learned as you train with a professional, but you will hone those skills once you are working for yourself. You will see firsthand how professionals act with the customer, how representing yourself, explaining job aspects, and resolving issues are best handled. We learn by paying attention, by watching and doing repeatedly. These fantastic customer service skills soon become second nature. Not only will you use them daily with your customers, but these talents and skills will be crucial anytime you are stumped by a problem.

You'll use these talents and skills when meeting with college professors regarding questions or concerns about your grades or projects...when interacting with your roommates—or their regrettable overnight guests...when dealing with a landlord who is slow to fix a leaky toilet...when dealing with coworkers in your future. And I literally could go on forever...

From employee to entrepreneur

On a nice sunny day in my second summer of cleaning windows for $3.35 an hour, I was cleaning the window in the Rochester mayor's office. His office manager came in and asked me, "Do you clean house windows on the side?" "Sure," I said in a very unsure tone. I had never thought of that. I wondered if I could do it by myself. I didn't have any tools of my own, and I didn't know how much to charge. At this point everything was very much over my head.

Like any new experience, something that feels foreign to you can be overwhelming. But if you approach the situation with confidence that first time, it will only become easier with each successive outing. {**Sweet Tip**} Have some confidence in yourself when you start. Don't let the fear prevent you from even trying.

She gave me her address, and after work I drove to her house to look at the job. I gave her a price of $60. I had no idea how to price a job. My quote was a total guess. I probably could have charged more than I did. But I was new to this and in complete *fake it 'til you make it* mode. Had I gone into my summer job knowing I would end up cleaning windows for myself, I would have asked the important questions, such as, "How much do I charge per window?" Again, this is just one

15

advantage you'll enjoy by taking a job in your chosen field with the sole purpose of learning as much as you can.

I bought some tools from the local janitorial supply store and entered the great unknown of cleaning windows on my own. I cleaned that woman's windows the following Saturday. She paid me with three fresh $20 bills. I had worked three hours for $60. That's $20 per hour! I remember driving home from that job, and all I could think about was the fact that I had just made $60 in three hours. It was so easy! I wanted to do it again.

My mind never worked the same after that. I had officially flipped the entrepreneurial switch in my brain. The realization that I could make $20 an hour instead of $3.35 was just mind blowing. That was a life-changing moment for me that I will never forget. All I had to do now was find more people who wanted me to clean windows for them. I didn't know how to do it, but I knew I had to do it. And so my journey began.

Preparation

First, I prepared. From my on-the-job training, I knew what I needed in terms of tools. I went back to the janitorial supply store and bought a few more squeegees and some ladders. There was no Internet back then, no cell phones, no GPS. So I couldn't MapQuest the addresses or order supplies online. (There's that wrinkly old man again...) But I was a young man chock-full of ambition, who had just given himself a $16-an-hour raise. For $20 an hour, I would use a map and find the addresses.

I had my bucket full of window cleaning tools and I was ready to conquer the world—well, clean the glass of the world anyway. Where did my start-up money come from? All of my supplies, tools, equipment, and car were paid for with the money I'd earned and saved working those lower-paying jobs I mentioned earlier.

Now that I had all of the proper equipment, I was officially working for myself. I didn't really think about what I was doing or how I was doing it. I just did it. Everyone I knew thought it was really cool that I was running around cleaning windows and making a sweet dime doing it. Note, however, that none of my friends wanted to give up their after-school TV time or weekends to do it...that's an illustration of the 90 and the 10. Of course I didn't see it that way at the time. Back then I was just a high school kid doing what he needed to do to make some cash. See, you can be the 10 and not even know it.

Next came advertising. I needed more customers. I didn't take out an ad in the phonebook or buy a month on a billboard. Heck, I didn't have the money or any idea how to do that. And, like I mentioned, there was no Internet—no websites, Facebook, or Craigslist. What I did to advertise was logical, simple, and cheap. I distributed flyers. I posted and handed out what seemed to be thousands of flyers. My flyers were simple. They said "Residential Window Cleaning. Call Geof White." And I included my home phone number and a picture of a window that I had drawn. (Yep, I drew it. Not cut-and-paste or drag-and-drop, but drawn with a good old-fashioned number 2 pencil.)

It worked!

Distributing flyers paid off. It really didn't take long, maybe a week, before I got my first phone call. I was excited and scared to death at the same time. At that point I had $20 per hour stuck in my head, and after working hard every day at $3.35 an hour I was ready to make some real cash. You see, after that first $20-an-hour job, I didn't want to make $3.35 anymore. My perception of my worth had changed. My standard quickly became $20 an hour. I'd given myself that raise, and I didn't want to give it back. Potential customers were calling, and I was thrown into all kinds of situations with customers. The customer service education that I had received while at my low-paying jobs really came in handy.

While in training I had encountered customers in office settings, in the mall, on the street, or in their homes. Some people were nice, and some were not. That's just the way it goes. People in different settings expect different behaviors. In an office setting, it was best to be polite and quiet. However, in someone's home I was more apt to carry on a lengthy conversation because people were much more interested in developing a personal relationship. This makes sense considering I was spending several hours in their most private and personal space: their home. Some of my customers became even more than just a paycheck; they became friends and mentors. Connie Gisel was one such customer.

Connie had gotten one of my flyers and very much appreciated clean windows. She had me over to her house three or four times a year to keep them that way. I remember she had a dog, a boxer that wore a green collar with Louie Gisel on it. I would clean Connie's inside windows first. After the insides were all sparkle and shine, I'd hop outside and clean the exterior glass. As I cleaned the outsides, Louie would follow me from room to room, window to window. With every room and every window, Louie left a big wet and drippy nose print on the inside glass as he stared at me intently. Connie would say, "If he doesn't make that print now, he'll just do it later." But, wanting to provide the best possible customer service, I quickly changed my routine. For future visits I cleaned the outsides first and made sure to remove Louie's personal stamp of approval from the insides later. Problem solved. *Another lesson: don't be afraid to change your ways to improve your system.* {**Sweet Tip**}

Connie was a great customer. She was the sweetest lady, had fairly simple windows to clean, and she would feed me. Oh, yeah, feed me. Now what makes a person's day (especially a constantly hungry teenage boy) more than being paid and fed at the same job? I'm pretty sure that's having your cake and eating it too... almost literally. With Connie's cooking, it was like being paid twice.

She worked during the day, so she always had me come clean in late afternoon or on a weekend. After Louie and I would finish our window waltz, I'd make my way to the back porch. Connie, her husband Brad, Louie, and I would all sit down and eat dinner—usually spaghetti. Sometimes when I think back, I can still taste Connie's famous spaghetti.

Jean Massare was another customer I remember. I had put out flyers in her suburb. It was a good area to advertise in because it had larger homes with lots of windows. It was also close to where I lived. I didn't know it then, but I was targeting demographics by picking areas that were both close to my home and where my most-likely customers lived. I received several calls from that batch of flyers, and Jean was one. She had some tall windows in her house that overlooked a huge wooded ravine. This was the focal point of the house, so she liked to keep those windows clean. I always cleaned the inside and outside of those monsters. Outside I had to ladder off the porch, which was built on the side of the ravine. I would be on the top of a twenty-foot ladder looking down eighty feet into the woods below. The view was amazing and the windows weren't too difficult once I got up there...a perfect combination.

The first time I visited Mrs. Massare's house, she asked me where I went to school. I told her McQuaid Jesuit High School, which immediately made her eyes widen. She told me that her son also attended McQuaid but was a couple of years younger and that her daughter went to the same school as my little sister. Small world, right? She was ecstatic to help out a McQuaid boy by hiring me to clean her windows. (There's that Kid Card again.) Keep this example in mind when you're starting out. *Don't be afraid to develop a personal relationship with your customers.* {**Sweet Tip**}

After a while I cleaned the windows of almost every house on Mrs. Massare's street. It turned out that she was kind of like the neighborhood lookout. If there was a barbecue happening on that street or a car accident in the area, Jean had the details. She was on a first-name basis with everyone on the street and, luckily for me, she told everyone what a great job I did on her windows. Why did she do that? Because I did a good job. It's as simple as that.

If I had done a poor job, if I was late, or if I had a bad attitude, then she might have spread the word *not* to hire me. That's an important lesson and one you should learn early on. Satisfied customers will bring you more business. So do a good job. Do your best job. Exceed their expectations. Make the best damn lemonade around.

I remember how I would pull up on one end of the street in that neighborhood around 8:00 a.m. I'd park my car, pull out my gear, and clean windows until five or six o'clock at night. Then I'd come back the next day. I would clean maybe six or eight houses in two days. Every one of those houses was in the $175 to $250 price range. So if we take the low end, $175 per house, and multiply that by six, we have $1,050 in two days! That was enough to pay for a full trimester of college tuition—in two days). All that because I first handed out some flyers in a targeted neighborhood and exceeded one customer's expectations by being courteous, showing up on time, and cleaning a few bathroom mirrors for free.

By the time I was a senior in high school I had figured out how to bid jobs and how to work so efficiently that those $20-per-hour jobs were rare. At this point I almost always made $50 an hour, and that adds up fast when you have virtually no expenses. After all, I lived at home with my mom and younger sister. No rent, no food bill. I just paid for gas, concert tickets, and squeegee rubbers. So there I was, *Geof White, the Window Cleaner*. In fact, that's what I would say when I called customers. "Hello, this is Geof White, the window cleaner, returning your call. How can I help you?"

Learn from my mistakes

After high school graduation, I attended Michigan State University in East Lansing, Michigan. I became Geof White, the Spartan. When I arrived at school, I started taking low-paying jobs again. *Big mistake!* I didn't have the customer base that I'd established in Rochester and didn't know the area all that well, so unfortunately I let those things stop me from continuing on my profitable window cleaning path.

Often I'd make the weekend trip from Michigan back to New York, clean some windows, and then return to school on Monday for class. Usually I'd make enough on those trips to not only pay for the trip itself, but pay for a few weeks of school living. My big mistake was I didn't put out flyers in East Lansing. I didn't network. I didn't hand out business cards and ask for referrals. I didn't serve the best damn lemonade in town in East Lansing; I didn't serve anything! I signed on the dotted line. I took the student loan, I worked low-paying jobs, and I regret it.

I wish I had started cleaning windows again when I arrived at college. I just fell into the easy, low-paying job cycle again. That's how easy it is to be an employee. Even with my experience, I started working for someone else...until people in the office building where I was the maintenance guy saw me cleaning windows and were impressed. They were impressed enough to hire me to clean their house windows. I didn't have to go find the opportunity; it found me. I'm not kidding. Opportunities are everywhere!

Foolishly I just cleaned their windows and did not pursue referrals. I took window cleaning jobs when they came in, but never pursued the opportunities like I had in high school. I was a complete jackass! I had the tools and the knowledge and did nothing with them in East Lansing. I could have asked for referrals. I could have played the college Kid Card. I could have been the best damn window cleaner in East Lansing. But I didn't. You know why? I was tricked by the ease of the student loans, lulled into acceptance of living off the loans. The student loans made it easy; they gave me a false sense that everything was being paid for.

I paid for my college education myself. No family help at all. And if you are in the same boat, you know how stressful and challenging it is. Although I did take out some student loans, I had no other financial support. If I sound proud of this fact, that's because I am. Putting yourself through college financially is a huge accomplishment any way you slice it, and if you can make $50 an hour it's much less painful to write that tuition check every semester. If you make $8 an hour, you might not be able to write the check at all. You'll know exactly what I'm talking about in a year or so after you are out there working for yourself.

The total cost for my college education was somewhere in the $40,000 to $50,000 range, including classes, room and board, car expenses, and all that other stuff that comes along with college. (It's important to note that this cost is now $85,000+.) Isn't that kind of sad? Such a huge investment, a really large amount of money, and I cannot remember exactly how much it was. See how easily money and the cost of things can get away from you? I graduated with $15,000 in student loans. (Looking back that number should have been $0). My little sister, Natalie, who is now a doctor, went to Michigan State as well. However, we paid for college two different ways. She took out student loans and worked low-paying jobs, whereas I borrowed, worked some low-paying jobs, and worked for myself.

Natalie had wanted to be a doctor ever since she was helping me with my lemonade stand as a kid, and I have to commend her for doing it with no family financial help whatsoever. With the same financial disadvantage I had, she always had to work. She had jobs as a waitress, babysitter, security guard, fish monger… okay, no fish mongering. And of course she had student loans. Don't forget, to become a doctor takes a lot more work, time, and money than your typical four-year degree. So her student loan bill was significantly higher when she graduated. It was ten times my student loan bill. Yes, she graduated with a six-figure student loan. Ouch! Even more painful is how common that really is.

I remember one blistering summer day when the differences between our methods of making money became very apparent. It was one of those hot humid days when it seemed like anything and everything would melt. At any moment I expected to see a Dali-like clock dripping down the wall. I was home from college for summer break and cleaning windows every day. Natalie was about to start her senior year in high school. Each of us finished with work at the same time, somewhere around four o'clock. We lumbered in the house and plopped down on the couch. We were both dog-tired in the dog days of summer.

Natalie was working as a security guard at the time. This meant she sat at a desk and read books all day, waiting for someone to walk up and sign in. Natalie was an avid reader and studier. This job was quite well suited to her since it allowed her to get paid to read. The only problem was that she made like $5 or $6 an hour sitting at that desk. I, on the other hand, had just cleaned the outside windows of a very large house owned by an attorney in town. I'd probably lost a few pounds due to how much I sweated. The house took me two days to complete. Two days to clean just the outside windows of a house in the heat of summer is a very long time, but my payment at the end of those two days was $900! It was a job well worth the effort.

So we were sitting there—me with a large glass of ice water, Natalie with an ice cream sandwich—and I asked her, "How much did you make today?" She took a bite of her ice cream and through a mouthful said, "I don't know, forty dollars." I pulled out nine one-hundred-dollar bills and said, "I made $450 today and $450 yesterday." She made a face, told me to shut up, and threw the remainder of her ice cream sandwich at me. I'm pretty sure it hit me on the forehead and then slowly dripped down and landed in my water as I sat there in a state of shock. Yeah, I deserved it. I'm not saying I worked any harder than she did that day, though physically I probably did.

The point I'm trying to get across is that we both spent all day working. I came home with $450 and she came home with $40. The difference was that I found a customer willing to pay me $450 for nine hours of work, and she found an employer willing to pay her $40. My poor little sister put up with a lot of my shenanigans. But you know what? Kudos to her! She put herself through medical school with absolutely no help. She worked years of low-paying jobs and took out plenty of student loans to accomplish her long-term goal. She became the doctor she always wanted to be.

Well, that's my story. I started cleaning windows at the age of sixteen. By seventeen I was working for myself. I was the boss; I did things my way. I kept at it through college and paid my own way. That was my lemonade stand. I served up my own recipe, and customers seemed to really like it. I strove to become the best damn window cleaner around so I could charge enough to pay for college.

You can do the same thing. Earning your own money and paying for things yourself is awesome. I took some detours and hit some bumps along the way. By sharing them with you, I hope you won't run into the same problems. But if you do, you'll know better how to handle them. Next we'll be looking at the true cost of college and getting you started on the path to working less, making more, and becoming the 10.

CHAPTER 2

When life gives you lemons, take 'em. Free lemons! No interest!

Debt is a four-letter word

Total outstanding student loan debt in America has passed $1 trillion, exceeding the nation's credit card debt. Equally alarming, average indebtedness per student is rising. This is especially scary since most graduates carry both student loan debt *and* credit card debt. But that's not what college is supposed to be about. College is about learning and investing in your future by way of higher education and the college experience. College does more for a young adult than just provide a degree. It helps you build character and learn problem-solving and coping skills. College provides a student the platform to display unique talents and views.

The college experience is something that I found priceless in every area: the friends, the education, the fun, the life lessons. It's a pivotal time in any young adult's life and I am trying to show you how to lessen the burden—debt—that often comes along with the college experience. This financial burden can haunt you for years or possibly decades.

More often than not, your first job out of college will start you at the bottom of that profession's pay scale. Don't assume because you're a college graduate that you won't have to start at the bottom. It's like being a freshman all over again, and it can take years to advance on the pay scale. On top of that, even if your student loan payment is relatively small, chances are that you'll end up repaying almost twice as much as you borrowed. Typically your student loan payments can be deferred for six months, meaning you have a grace period during which you don't have to make payments...yet. Depending on what type of loan you have, however, it may be accruing interest during the grace period so you'll owe even more money. Additionally recent adjustments to student loan repayment laws mean that your first payment may be due as soon as sixty days after graduation—before you even get your diploma in the mail!

Before we get any further into this discussion of pay scales, debt, credit, and loans, let's keep in mind that money and debt are now mostly numbers on a computer screen. We are becoming a global cashless society, and there's no turning back. What does this mean? It means that the debt you have looks and feels like just a number on a bank statement...easily disregarded, easily procrastinated about, easily put off until you *have the money*. You can defer loans for only so long. Once your deferments run out, so does your luck. That's when you have no choice but to start repaying. And guess what? Unless you win the lottery, the chance of your writing a big check to pay off the balance in full is about as good as winning the lottery itself.

It's hard to get rich quick, and it's even harder to get out of debt quick. Take that as you will, but just remember the money game is set up by banks in the best interest of the banks. Those who are lending the money aren't necessarily in it for your best interest. The more you borrow and the longer you take to pay back your loan, the more money the lenders make. Your wallet gets thinner while theirs gets fatter. It's a gradual process so you might not feel as much pain in the beginning, which benefits the lender. When you graduate and write that first monthly $250 loan payment check, you don't realize that only a portion applies to the principal.

Why work so hard to graduate with no debt? Why not just go to college, take out a student loan, and pay it off after graduation when you are making the big bucks? "If I owe $20,000 after graduation," you think, "and I'm making $41,000, I'll just pay my debt off right away. Right?" Wrong! Easier said than done. If you get a job after graduation that pays $41,000 a year, which was the national average in 2010 according to the National Center for Educational Statistics (NCES), that $41,000 is gross income. Gross income is the amount of money you make before any taxes are taken out.

For those of you who have not experienced a paycheck from an employer yet, there is an initial shock when you look at that first paycheck. Say you worked at the corner store making $8 an hour for twenty hours last week. Twenty hours times $8 would be $160, right? That is your gross pay, but that is not what your paycheck will be. Your paycheck will be somewhere around the amount of $136, which is your net pay, commonly called take-home pay. Thus the initial shock of your first paycheck. Where did the other $24 go? That's three hours of work right there! The government will withhold a certain amount of every paycheck for Social Security and federal, state, and local income taxes. The amount withheld can vary from state to state and also depends on how much you ask to be taken out. So when you get that first job out of college, after taxes you aren't making $41,000; you're bringing home more like $37,000.

You are also assuming you find a job in your profession right away. Hopefully you won't have to work at that corner store while you are in limbo looking for that first *real* job out of college. Also take into consideration that it's now common for interviewers to ask college graduates about their student loan burden during the interview process. This helps them determine if you can realistically work for the entry-level wages they are offering. Sometimes the pay offered is not enough to cover living expenses with the addition of a large student loan. The fact that you took out loans with the long-term goal of getting a better job may actually be a deciding factor keeping you from that job. So you can see why it's important to make wise financial decisions now because, after college graduation, you aren't running a lemonade stand anymore and your mom isn't buying your cups and sugar.

Here are some disturbing stats to chew on. There are typically five job seekers for each job opening according to the Bureau of Labor Statistics. Fewer than half (44 %) of employers planned to hire new college grads in 2010 according to a 2010 CareerBuilder survey. That's down from 79 % in 2007. Not very promising when you take into account that about 2.4 million students graduated with either a bachelor's or associate's degree in 2010 according to the NCES. Do you feel like a number now? Well, don't be one. And if you are a number, be the 10! Differentiate yourself from those other 2.4 million job applicants on your resume and in your wallet.

It's fairly common for college graduates to wait tables or take low-paying jobs for several months or years before they find a job in their chosen profession. This is another reason to work for yourself in college. You can carry it forward into that post-graduation limbo period. By doing so, you can continue making more money than you would in one of those low-paying jobs or at least add some cash to your weekly paycheck at that steady lower-paying job.

According to a poll by collegegrads.com, 80% of college graduates (up from 67% in 2006) move back in with their parents after graduation. Let's face it, nobody wants that to happen—not you and not your parents! It took me three months to find a job after college graduation, and that job was somewhat different than what I had studied for. However, all the business skills I learned working for myself and the knowledge I gained in college classes still applied, just to a different profession. Sometimes that first job out of college is in an area that was completely off your radar while you were in the midst of the college experience. Maybe a little leap of faith is required after college. You never know; you may like your new situation and stick with it.

Recent NCES statistics show:
The average high school graduate earns in the range of
$18,000 – $25,000 per year,
The average college graduate (Bachelor's degree) earns in the range of
$37,000 – $45,000 per year.

NCES statistics also state that even when unemployment rates are high, the unemployment rates for those with a Bachelor's degree are consistently lower than the national average.

For the purpose of this chapter we will use the median incomes of:
$21,000 for high school graduates
$41,000 for college graduates

The debt cycle

Once you start a debt cycle, it's very hard to break. Say you go to a private college and borrow $15,000 a year for four years. That means you'd graduate with $60,000 in student loan debt. Let's say the interest rate is 6.8%. To repay this loan in ten years, you would be dropping seven Benjamins a month! For those of you a little less hip (parents), that's $700 per month for ten years! At that rate you'd pay a total of $83,000 over the ten-year period. If you go twenty years on that same $60,000 debt, it would cost you $460 a month; and you would end up paying $110,000. (Nearly three times your annual income at your first job after graduation!) Not to mention the fact that you very realistically could still be making payments on your student loan when your own children start college…and take out their first student loans. I don't know about you, but I don't want to give away $27,000; and I certainly don't want to be making a $700 monthly student loan payment at age thirty-two, much less a $460 payment at age forty-two.

The national average is $24,000 total debt per student coming out of college. If you pay that off in ten years, the payment would be $280 per month for a total payback of $33,000. If you take twenty years to pay off the same $24,000, it would be $185 per month with a total payback of $45,000, which is almost double what you borrowed in the first place. Double? Really? This is the exact conversation your parents should be having with you, but many are not. I wish my mom had explained it to me before I started college. Instead I learned it the hard way after graduation by way of a big fat bill every month.

Life (and expenses) after graduation

Let's look at the debt issue after graduation. For our scenario you'll have a student loan with a $280 per month payment. You have graduated from a good four-year college. You have a good job in the profession of your choice, and you needed that college education to get that job so it's worth the $280 per month. Of course that $41,000 annual income isn't guaranteed and can fluctuate drastically depending on your field of study, specific entry-level position, and geographic location. The cost of living fluctuates between different areas of the country. For example, the architect in a small Midwest city may not make nearly as much as an architect in New York City, simply due to the difference in the cost of living for those particular areas. Housing prices, taxes, and population all play a role in determining the cost of living. It's not something to get hung up on, but you should be aware of it when you consider job offers.

At this point $41,000 may seem like plenty to live on and make your monthly student loan payment, but there are other expenses and debts you will incur upon graduation that need to be considered. Just like the sticker shock of college tuition, there is a sticker shock for adult life, too.

First, you need something to drive. And with your new job, you don't want to drive a *beater* anymore. So you find a decent used Lexus. There's another $300-per-month payment. Your insurance has now gone up drastically because you can no longer be on your parents' policy. Yet you are still in your twenties, the age for which auto insurance rates are at their highest, so there's another good $100-a-month bill. Now there's a girlfriend or boyfriend involved, and you buy a $400 German shepherd together. Now you're spending an extra $100 per month on dog food and the occasional vet bill.

You can't live in a dinky little college apartment with a dog, so what do you do? You rent or buy a small house, the American dream in all its glory. That old college furniture as well as the obligatory neon beer signs just don't look right in your new home. So you're off to the furniture store to spend much more than you were expecting to pay for a couch, love seat, and end tables. Now you still have the student loan payment of $280 per month, but additionally you have: $200 for health insurance, $300 for your now not-so-decent Lexus that needs a repair here and there, and $1,000 for your mortgage or rent. You've got the heat, water, electricity, cable/Internet, and cell phone bills. Let's just list all the expenses and see what it costs a month once you graduate and real-life finances slap you in the face. And try not to cry.

Monthly Bills

Rent or Mortgage...........	....$1,000
Heat/Water/Electricity ...	....$300
Car Payment..................	....$300
Car Insurance	....$100
Gas for the car...............	....$200 ($50/wk)
Health Insurance............	....$200
Renters Insurance...........	....$20
Cable/Internet................	....$100
Cell phone	....$100
Food..............................	....$400 ($100/wk)
Pet Expenses..................	....$100
Eating out......................	....$400
	($100/wk = one nice dinner out and some lunches)
Clothes...........................	....$50
Student Loan..................	....$280

**Total of $3,650/month or $43,800/year
(that's also = $842/week)**

Remember you are only bringing home $37,000 a year. You are already upside-down financially by $6,800. Good luck writing that big check to pay off your student loans! You are having trouble writing the $280-per-month student loan check because you are now $567 short a month. Next thing you know, it's a few years after graduation and the student loan bill comes every month and gets thrown on the pile of bills that just seems to grow. Remember, this list doesn't even include variable costs like vacations, holidays, additional furniture, auto repairs, hobbies, saving for retirement, and buying your nephew a birthday gift.

And if you have children, your monthly expenses can go up significantly. These are all real expenses once you graduate.

At the age of eighteen, when you are heading off to college, you are not thinking of monthly bills or your cost of living; and you shouldn't be. But you must be aware of these things and spend at least a little time now thinking about them. Your expenses will grow as you get older, and that is where debt trouble develops. *It's not any one single loan or bill that will bury you. It's the combination of all the little loans that will make you feel like your drowning.* [**Sweet Tip**] It's that car that you owe more on than it's worth; it's that $3,000 medical insurance deductible that you have to pay from when you twisted your knee and needed surgery. Maybe it will be the 3D television and holographic projector wired into your smart apartment or smartpartment. It will cost a lot to have that thing project life-size images and be voice-activated. On top of that, you might need the magneto-bed that lets you literally sleep on air. That won't be cheap either.

So what happens in order to make all of these payments? First you start not saving for retirement because you have bills to pay. When tapping into what you would normally pay into a retirement fund—hopefully a Roth IRA or matching 401(k) plan—no longer covers it, you start tapping into your emergency savings (if you have any). Without warning another incident happens and suddenly you're paying bills with a credit card that charges 21% interest. It doesn't matter what the calamity is or will be. Maybe your dog develops appendicitis or your refrigerator dies. Either way you don't have the funds available to pay for it; so you borrow more, thus strengthening the debt cycle that is now running your life.

All of a sudden, but also very gradually, that $280-per-month student loan is much harder to pay than you ever expected. That student loan payment becomes low priority in the increasing stack of bills, and you know what happens to the bill at the bottom of the pile. It doesn't get paid because you ran out of money that month.

 In 2007, *College seniors with at least one credit card graduated with an average of $4,138 in card debt, up 44% from 2004.*

Credit cards

Credit card companies bombard college students with all kinds of offers, introductory rates, cash-back bonuses, and the like. But read that fine print. Once your tempting, low interest introductory rate is gone and they've upped your credit limit from $500 to $2,500, that's when you get into trouble. Now is the time for willpower, discipline, and intelligence. It's easy to whip that credit card out in an *emergency* like...it's Sunday night and you are starving and want a piping-hot pizza delivered to your door in thirty minutes or less. Your three roommates need to eat, too. And you need a two-liter bottle of Dew to get you through the long night of studying. And bread sticks! Oh, how you love those bread sticks. Pretty soon that $9.99 pizza costs $50...and weeks after your last roommate burps the alphabet, that credit card bill with the $50 pizza charge on it is due.

If you have a credit card or plan on getting one, be careful. Credit cards can be used wisely, such as for actual emergencies, for online purchases, or to keep track of business purchases (expenses). *An excellent way to start out in the whole credit game is to go to a credit union, not a bank, and apply for a secured student credit card with a low limit that also has a relatively low interest rate. Then don't use it.* [Sweet Tip] A secured credit card means that you pay for the credit limit up front. If the credit limit is $500 you pay the institution $500 right away before you even use the card. With an unsecured credit card (which is more common and probably what your parents have in their wallets), you are borrowing the money from the bank that issued the credit card to be paid back later. In other words...debt.

Keep your credit card for actual emergencies or strictly for online orders. Never use it for impulse purchases. I have heard of people who keep their credit cards in the freezer in a baggie of ice, so they can't use them until they're thawed out. Thus they think about the purchase, and it prevents them from buying on impulse. The golden rule of credit cards is to always pay the full balance at the end of the month. If you pay anything less than the full statement balance, you will start accruing interest charges. If you pay off the balance in full each month, you will not pay any interest. By using the card only for emergencies or for business purchases, you'll be building your credit for that future time when you do in fact need credit, like when you need a mortgage for a house or an auto loan. The last thing you want to do is start going out to eat every day and charging it.

I suggested going to a credit union because, in general, credit unions are a much wiser place to take your financial matters. Credit unions are owned by their members so they retain their profits, whereas a bank returns profits to its shareholders. In 2008 one of the largest banks in the United States incorrectly charged overdraft fees that were in the billions. That means hundreds of thousands of unsuspecting folks were incorrectly charged those horrid fees that are sometimes more than $30 per overdraft item. Choose a local credit union, and you will be less likely to get overcharged or run into mistakes with your transactions. A credit union will also be more likely to help you in the future with auto loans, mortgages, and business loans if you have been a member for a while. I still utilize the credit union I used in college for auto loans because its interest rates are low and its underwriting is more forgiving due to the length of time I've been a member.

For those readers who don't know, underwriting is the department in a financial institution that either approves or declines your loan application. This department takes into consideration your income, monthly expenses, current debt level, how much money you need, your credit score, and how long you have done business with the institution. As you can see, all the different aspects of personal finances come together at times in your life, especially with big purchases. This is a good reason to establish a good relationship with your credit union early. In fact, I just recently took out an auto loan for a work truck and used the same credit union I used in college. This institution has great rates, and the people there value my membership because I have been with them so long.

You can retire with what could have been your student loan payment

Say you did not borrow to go to college and you have now graduated. You read *Lemonade Stand Economics*, became the 10, worked for yourself to pay for college, and have no student loan at all. Congratulations! Now here's a killer idea for you. *Take the amount of money you would have used to pay off a student loan after graduation and put it into a Roth IRA retirement account.* {**Sweet Tip**} Let's use that $280-per-month would-be payment and deposit it into a Roth IRA every month, earning 7% interest. After ten years you have paid in $33,000, but the value of your account would be $49,000 due to the accrued interest. This means you made $16,000 in interest. Say you keep putting that same $280 into that Roth IRA every month until you are 65. Guess how much you will have then? $857,000! Yes, almost a million dollars sitting there waiting for you at retirement. Did I mention that any funds you withdraw from a Roth IRA are completely tax-free? Yup, $857,000 of tax-free money. And how much did that $857,000 actually cost you out-of-pocket over the years? $141,000. Because you started contributing at such a young age, the compound interest added $716,000 of free money to your account. I'll take $716,000 of free money all day long! You can actually go one step further. If you do not spend all $857,000 in that first year of retirement, which realistically you shouldn't, then the remainder will sit in that account collecting more interest. A year of 7% interest on $857,000 is $62,000. You could possibly live off the interest alone in retirement.

The previous paragraph makes me sick to my stomach. Seriously. What an idiot I was! It was that easy for me to pay for college, graduate with no debt, and simply stick $280 a month into a Roth IRA; and I didn't do it. The sad part is that no one told me about this when I was eighteen; but frankly I don't know that I would have listened if they had. I was that hyper-independent kid who thought he knew everything. Maybe you are, too. Maybe you know everything. And if you do, you know that $857,000 is a life-changing amount of money; and putting away $280 a month isn't that much when you're making $50 an hour. Again, please *learn from my mistakes*

Public or private

If you're picking up this book, then you're smart enough to choose the right college for you. I chose Michigan State University because I was interested in the university's Building Construction Management program. High school graduates pick a certain college for all sorts of reasons, like academics, sports programs, location, or the cost of the school. Unfortunately that *cost of the school* is becoming the number one reason students choose a college. Hopefully you also have other reasons for choosing your college, but affordability is still an issue. When it comes to the cost of college there are some differences that you should be aware of.

Public universities, also called state schools, get funding from government sources and generally have lower tuition than private schools. State schools are funded partially by the state and federal governments, much like public high schools.

Private schools on the other hand receive their funding solely from tuition, philanthropists, alumni donations, and various fees. As a general rule, expect to pay more for a private school than a public one. There are also cases where a private school may actually cost less than a state school when specific students qualify for scholarships or grants for attending the private school. But as a general rule of thumb, that public university will cost less to attend.

Recent NCES statistics show:
The average annual cost for a student to attend college
Private $35,500   ($142,000 for four years)
Public $18,900   ($75,600 for four years)

Of course these are averages. Some state schools (or private for that matter) may be double the average price or half the average depending on the school. These average public university costs are in-state tuition rates. In-state tuition is the rate that a student pays when he or she lives in and graduated from a high school in the same state as the chosen public university. Out-of-state students will pay a higher rate, often double the in-state tuition. The NCES college cost figures I cited earlier include books, fees, tuition, housing, and a basic college meal plan. They *do not* include eating out, clothing, laundry, study abroad costs, transportation costs, cell phones, or anything associated with fun. And college should have an element of fun!

Obviously choosing a school is a very personal decision for you and your parents to make. If you plan to study hyperdimensional physics, tetrahedral geometry and holography, getting into one of the top private institutions might be the right choice for you. If you aren't going in that direction and plan to be an entrepreneur, my experience has taught me that success has more to do with discipline, ambition, perseverance, and a little bit of creativity than which college you attend. The real key here is to pick the school *you* want to attend, the school that matches your goals for educational and personal reasons. As it relates to paying for school, much of your plan for combining work and school is contingent upon the public/ private decision.

The cost of college has increased tenfold since 1979. A degree that cost $10,000 to earn in 1979 costs $100,000 now.

Financial aid and student loans

Financial aid is a very broad term that includes student loans, grants, and scholarships. If there is any way to qualify for grants or scholarships, do it. It's free money for school. Student loans must be repaid, but not scholarships and grants. While student loans are easy to apply for by simply filling out the loan application, scholarships and grants will require a little more work on your part. Student loans exist purely to assist the student with paying for college, right? Not really. A student loan serves two purposes. First, it enables a student to attend college that he or she otherwise could not afford. Second, it makes money for the lender. While I don't have a problem with banks making money by loaning money to students—after all banking is a business—I do have a problem with loans becoming the standard for financing most students' college education. Thankfully most college students utilize a mix of several of the funding sources noted above.

Student loans are exactly what they sound like. They are loans given to students to finance their education. They are sold as *an investment in your future*, and I don't disagree with that. A college degree is absolutely an investment in your future. Higher education will bring a higher paycheck and most likely a higher quality of life after graduation. However, I object to the fact that there is more emphasis from our government to just take out student loans vs. encouraging students to work to pay for college while they attend. Each of the various forms of financial aid has its place. Let's take a look at all of them so you can decide which works best for your situation.

The Stafford Loan

The Stafford Loan is the most common of all the student loans. It comes subsidized or unsubsidized. My student loan was a subsidized Stafford Loan. For this loan you'll need to fill out the FAFSA or Free Application for Federal Student Aid (fafsa.ed.gov). In July of 2012, the laws changed regarding both subsidized and unsubsidized loans. They now carry a 6.8 % fixed interest rate. It may sound like a great thing to do, but again the ramifications of the debt after graduation can and will haunt you.

With the subsidized Stafford Loan, interest doesn't accrue until after graduation or deferment. Loan acceptance is not based on credit history, and the limit to which you can borrow is affected by what year you are in school and whether you have parental assistance in paying for school. With the subsidized Stafford Loan, you do not make any immediate payments. The federal government pays the interest while you're in school, during the deferment period after you graduate (now limited to 60 days), and for any additional authorized deferments. A deferment is when the lender allows to not to make payments for a period of time without penalty. Your loan will accrue interest during a deferment period, however. When you see that a Stafford Loan is subsidized by the US government, don't get excited; the government is not going to pay off your student loan for you if you don't pay it yourself. The subsidized part means that the underwriters of the loan can lower their lending standards in order to get you the loan in the first place. In fact, there is no way out of a student loan once you sign on the dotted line. If you file for bankruptcy at some point and figure you can get rid of your student loan that way, think again. A student loan cannot be charged off by filing bankruptcy.

The unsubsidized Stafford Loan is slightly different. The borrowing limit is higher in case you need more than the subsidized loan can offer. The unsubsidized Stafford Loan also accrues interest while you are enrolled in school, which means that as soon as you take out this loan your interest clock starts ticking. Much like the subsidized loan, the unsubsidized Stafford allows you to defer payments while you're enrolled in school; but once you graduate, the interest is thrown on top of what you borrowed. Doesn't seem like a good deal to me, but I guess for some it makes sense; and since the Stafford is need-based, you may not have the option of subsidizing.

The Pell Grant and scholarships

I took advantage of the Pell Grant as well as a small scholarship while in college. It was free money...of course I took it. It sure made things easier on me. The Pell Grant is a federal award based on need that doesn't require repayment. When you fill out the FAFSA application you are automatically in the running for a Pell Grant. So even if you aren't taking out a loan, it is in your best interest to fill out the FAFSA to see if you can indeed get the Pell.

Scholarships work the same way. Scholarships require a bit more work to get than the Pell Grant, though. You might have to write an essay or two and often the people awarding the scholarship want to know why you deserve the scholarship more than another person. Here's an excellent opportunity to practice your shameless self-promotion. A day or two spent working on getting a scholarship can save you a lot money, hard work, and headaches later on.

The thing about scholarships, much like earning opportunities, is that they are everywhere—some small and some large—but you still have to find them. Churches, civil organizations, business associations, and community groups all offer scholarships; and yes, of course, colleges offer them. Scholarships are often offered for certain talents. Everyone has heard about student athletes who get a *full ride* to a college to play sports there. Colleges also offer academic scholarships. You know those classmates as well, the ones who blow the bell curve all the time. My twelve-year-old son performs in a holiday show every year at school, and even the program has a college scholarship available. While all scholarships differ, many require that, once awarded the money, the student must reapply on a yearly basis. Some are performance-based, requiring you to keep a certain grade point average or maintain a certain sports position. Your Internet search should yield a greater knowledge of where scholarships can be found and how to apply for them. There are great scholarship apps available, too.

Hopefully you'll find something you qualify for. If you haven't yet, keep looking. The money is out there. You should definitely look into grants and scholarships before even thinking about taking out a loan. A simple Internet search for *college scholarships* will yield plenty of options to keep you busy. If you want more options, just search *free money for college* and read away. I will caution you, however, to read carefully. You should never pay up front for a grant or scholarship to be awarded to you. Nor should you pay a fee to have someone else complete and submit applications on your behalf. Be cautious and smart when it comes to Internet sources.

A lot of footwork is involved in tracking down and applying for scholarships, but being awarded a scholarship can be likened to working out once you actually force yourself to do it, it's really not too bad. You might even feel better after you're finished.

End of the doom and gloom

That's it. I'm through spewing the doom and gloom. You want to go to college, and I want you to go to college. We all know debt is bad. Now it's time to figure out a way to pay for college that doesn't include debt. If you do need to take out some loans, let's keep them to an absolute minimum. Aside from applying for every scholarship and grant that even remotely applies to you, it's time to make some money and pay for this college experience. I've often thought that the true test of college tenacity is not coursework completion or grades but how you managed getting to college and paying for it. Paying for college is no small feat. It's expensive. The fact that an eighteen-year-old kid can figure out a way to pay tens of thousands of dollars over a four-year span for that education is just as impressive as getting the degree itself. If I can do it, so can you. Let's get to work and make this happen.

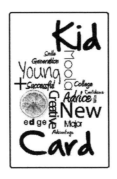

CHAPTER 3

Lemons do grow on trees, but they don't fall into your lap

From Lewis Carroll's *Alice's Adventures in Wonderland*:

> **Alice:** Would you tell me, please, which way I ought to go from here?
> **The Cat:** That depends a good deal on where you want to get to.
> **Alice:** I don't much care where.
> **The Cat:** Then it doesn't much matter which way you go.

Like Alice, if you don't know where you are going, it's hard to know where to start. *Your lemonade stand will be more successful tomorrow if you prepare for it today.* [**Sweet Tip**] Do you have all the lemonade ingredients? Do you have extra lemonade mix? Do you have enough cups? Did you check the weather forecast? Did you make the sign? Did you tell your neighbors about your soon-to-be stand? Where is that card table hiding? Do you have a few quarters for change? Does your mother even know you are going to open a lemonade stand?

The Gameplan

Your stakes are higher now than when you had that childhood lemonade stand. Much higher. You didn't need a plan of attack back then, just a sunny afternoon. This is different. You need to have blueprints before you can start building a house. And you need a blueprint before you work for yourself. You need a plan of attack, a Lemonade Stand Gameplan. I have Gameplan references throughout the book. There are times in this book when you should go to the Gameplan and input some information. I have indicated this throughout with the Gameplan icon I do this be- cause, while you may be think- ing a lot about a certain topic to- day, three weeks from now, after you haven't thought about that topic for a while, you may need to reference it. The Gameplan gives you a place to write it all down so you can refer to it later. I've included a Gameplan worksheet in the back of the book or you can download one from the website.

The Gameplan is simply a structured outline for your basic goals and how to achieve those goals. I will refer to it throughout the book whenever there is an opportunity to input information. It will walk you through each section. I know everyone hates the accompanying *workbook*, but just like a business plan it serves a purpose. Like a business plan, your Gameplan will include all of your goals and the step-by-step components to get there. Using a Gameplan now is also excellent practice for that business venture you may enter into years down the road. After all, if you start looking for opportunities at age seventeen, chances are you will be looking for opportunities at twenty-three, too.

You may have heard moans and groans about a business plan, but trust me, what we're talking about here is about as scary as a clown…unless of course you're terrified of clowns. The Gameplan needs to be simple, with realistic goals and realistic steps to achieve those goals. Your Gameplan will start with your financial goal of paying for college. You will then figure out how much you need to earn each day of the summer to achieve that goal. Then you will pick a service to provide. You will train, pick up side jobs, and then begin working for yourself. You will find customers and maximize efficiency. You will provide excellent customer service and learn business skills, all the while making good money. The Gameplan is the place to write down and see these goals and steps in black and white. In reality what you do and how you do it will inevitably change, twist and turn; but at this point we need to get you heading in the right direction.

The purpose of the Gameplan is to get all this information down on paper so you can take the right steps to accomplish your goals. Let's be real honest, though. A Gameplan is a great exercise before you start your business, but once you are into the venture you won't look at your Gameplan much. It's more of a tool to use in the beginning to make sure you are headed in the right direction, listing things you want to do, need to do, and don't want to forget. The initial Gameplan will look quite different from the Gameplan for year three or four. The long-term financial goal may be the same, but short-term goals and how they are achieved will change as time goes on and your skills improve. You should update the Gameplan at the beginning of every summer, but that doesn't mean a complete overhaul is necessary. Basically you want to review how the previous year went so that you can adjust your plan to make the upcoming year more productive.

Again, how much of this Gameplan you fill out is up to you. The Gameplan provides an excellent opportunity to involve your parents. It will show them how serious you are and, hopefully, clarify for them what your goals are and how you plan on achieving them. If your parents have a clear picture of your plans, they will be more able to assist you where needed.

We have already discussed the long-term financial goal. Now let's look at what it's going to take to get there.

 From NCES: By their junior or senior year of high school, more than 90 % of students reported having discussions with their parents about academic requirements or the type of college they hoped to attend. However, less than 50 % reported discussing college costs or financial aid.

A financial plan now or financial pain later

I wish I had made a financial plan to pay for college. I do regret that I didn't. I never sat down, figured out how much college was going to cost, figured out how much I needed to make, and implemented a lifestyle that was conducive to accomplishing my goal. Making this plan *before* you get to college is crucial. Once you set foot on campus, the game of life resets. It's a new world with new rules. Sensory and educational overload will commence.

When I arrived at Michigan State, I was overwhelmed with classes and socializing in my new setting. I was eight hours from home. I didn't know anybody. I was living with a roommate whom I had never met before in a city I had visited only twice in my life. Freshman year is exciting, scary, and overwhelming. That's why you want to get the financial aspect of paying for college figured out before you get to college. There are just too many distractions in your first year of college (good distractions, I might add) to be dealing with how you are going to pay for it. Besides, *it is so much easier if you can start your financial planning in high school when you have dear old Mom and Dad right there to help.* [Sweet Tip]

This brings me to another point. If your parents are from the school of *you're on your own, kid* and offer little help or advice when it comes to college or anything financial for that matter, then your road will be a bit rockier. But there is help out there. You just have to find it. There is your school counselor. (It's his or her job, right?) You can ask for advice from aunts, uncles, grandparents, your friends' parents, and people in church or community groups. It's been my experience that most adults are very happy to assist a teenager who needs financial advice.

So how much is this college degree going to cost? I know, I'm wincing too. I want to hear the number, but I don't want to hear the number. I know it's going to be big—and scary—and *big*. First, remember this college education with the big scary price tag is an investment, one of the most important investments you can make in yourself. It's not like buying shoes, where they end up worn out and thrown away after a time. You will get to keep and use this education for the rest of your life. It cannot be taken away. Many years down the road, it will benefit you in ways you can't even imagine now. Maybe you already have a certain university in mind, or maybe you have no clue where you will be attending. For the purpose of saving for college, a rough idea of cost is all you need. We are not counting out quarters to get to a certain number here. We are simply trying to be as financially prepared as possible so you can head off to your freshman year with the peace of mind that the year is paid for.

Every school has a different price to attend, and the price goes up every year. There are just too many variables to come up with an absolutely accurate number for every reader, so we will ballpark it. If you know the college you will be attending, then you already know your costs and should use those numbers. I would also add an additional 10%. Why? For those unexpected expenses. Even using the term *unexpected expenses* is laughable because you should *expect* those unexpected expenses. They will be there—you just don't know when, in what form, or how much they will cost until they actually come up. For our purposes we will simply use the national averages from private and public universities, plus an additional 10%. Once we know the cost, we can set our financial goal.

As we know from chapter 2, the national average cost to attend a public university per year is $18,900, meaning that by graduation you have paid (or borrowed) $75,600 for a BS/BA degree. The national average for a private university is $35,500 per year or $142,000 for a BS/BA degree. Having read those statistics, add 2 % per year over the statistical cost because universities raise their prices every year. So we're talking $75,600 for a degree? Yep, and we haven't even added the 10% for unexpected expenses and the annual 2% inflationary increase yet!

You can see how so many people get into debt paying for college. That's a large sum of money to save up. Although not impossible, I might add. We will use $20,000 per year as the cost of a public university since it's a nice round number to work with. Now let's add the 10% so the number we will be working with for the remainder of this exercise is $22,000a year. Again, depending on which particular school you attend, this $22,000 could be high or low. In some circumstances a state school might cost far less than the average, and if you mix in a grant or scholarship it can be quite a bit lower. Grants and scholarships can significantly decrease the cost of a school whether you choose public or private. For our purposes we will use the national average, so now we are talking about a four-year degree from a public college costing a total of $88,000. That is the goal and the amount you need to make before graduation. No problem! Yeah, I said no problem. That $88,000 is a huge, ugly, daunting, number…it's also very doable.

The first thing we need to do is get that ominous $88,000 price tag broken down into a manageable and palatable number so it won't freak a lot of people out. Let's break that $88,000 back down to $22,000 annually. After all, you have some time to do this. You don't need to write an $88,000 check right away freshman year. If you are reading this as a high school sophomore, for instance, you have three summers to work before you even head off to college, not to mention that you will have another three summers while in college before your senior year. So a high school sophomore has six summers to make $88,000. Let's do the math. You will need to make $14,666 a summer, which comes down to making $1,222 a week each week of the summer break. I know you don't want to work every day of the summer break. Nobody does. But unfortunately you don't have parents who are paying for your college degree, so working all summer break is just what you have to do. Remember work ethic? Time to prove to the world you have it.

If you work five days a week all summer, then you need to make $244 a day. How are you possibly going to make $244 a day for every day of the summer? First, we haven't even discussed working during the school year. Add working just two Saturdays a month during the school year to the mix, and you're down to needing to make $188 per day for every day you work whether it's a Saturday during the school year or a workday during summer break. You need to make $188 per day for five days a week in the summer and two Saturdays a month during the school year. To make $188 a day at $8 per hour would take you 23.5 hours each work day, which is obviously impossible. If you want to make more money you will need to increase either the amount of time you work or your rate of pay or both. I gave myself a raise by working harder, smarter, and finding more work. I increased my dollars per hour as well as increased how many hours I worked. *A six-day work week isn't going to kill you!* [**Sweet Tip**]

Setting goals

It's easy to set a goal. Yet after you set the goal, you have a tendency to forget about it. If a goal is not fresh in your mind, it simply isn't a goal anymore. During their busy day-to-day activities, people tend to forget what they are working so hard for. One suggestion is to keep one main goal and one daily goal visible at all times. Some people put their goals on the fridge...but I wouldn't. No one ever looks at their goals on the fridge. Instead I have two yellow sticky notes with written goals on my computer screen. The sticky note with my daily goal says, "Be absolutely prepared for tomorrow." The other note is my annual revenue goal. *Most everyone spends hours a day looking at his or her computer, so this is a perfect spot to put your goals. The more you look at the note, the more the goal will seep into your psyche. It will be at the top of your mind.* [**Sweet Tip**]

 Federal minimum wage is $7.25 per hour. Among employed teenagers aged 16-19 paid by the hour, 47.1% earn minimum wage or less according to the Bureau of Labor Statistics, 2010.

A note from the author: If you are the 10, please disregard this stat because it's not relevant to you.

$50 an hour vs. $8 an hour

All of the debt, the interest, and the post-graduation student loan stress completely disappear if you earn enough money along the way. And I assure you, you *can* earn enough to pay for college ahead of time. This goes against everything society has ingrained in us, but that doesn't make it less true. You know the theory we all grew up with: buy it now, pay for it later. But that isn't how it should or has to be.

What you need to do first is focus on your dollars per hour. The amount of money you can make per hour is crucially important when working for yourself. You want to earn as much per hour as possible, thus maximizing each hour of work.

I once heard it said that everyone is comfortable making a certain amount of money each year, whether it be $18,000 or $50,000 or $250,000. You will stop working hard once you achieve that goal, or if you are below that goal you will work like crazy to get to it. So why not make yourself comfortable at $50 an hour instead of $8 an hour? I know it sounds odd, especially if you are used to making $8 an hour, but listen to me. When I did that first job on my own for $20 an hour, I learned real fast to adjust my earning standards. And so will you.

By picking a niche service and becoming very proficient at it, you can make $15 or $25 or, some of you, even that coveted $50 an hour. Keep in mind that you can only attain $50 an hour *if you find customers willing to pay you that much* and *you offer a level of service deserving of that amount.* {Sweet Tip} When I talk about the *best damn lemonade in town,* what I mean is that, if you are asking for a premium price, the customer will expect a premium product. That customer will expect the best damn lemonade in town. When I was charging $50 an hour, I was the best damn window cleaner in town. I paid very close attention to every aspect of my service, so I exceeded my customers' expectations. Finding customers to pay $25 or $15 an hour is much easier. Yes, I said easier. In fact, working for yourself and finding jobs that pay you $15 an hour is quite easy. Remember, at $15 an hour, you are still making almost double what your friend, the sandwich artist, is making. I will explain later how to achieve these rates of pay, but for now let's get a good grasp on how that higher dollar-per-hour rate will affect your goal of coming up with $88,000 for college.

The dollars per hour you earn will affect how much time you will need to work to accomplish your financial goal. The graph below shows how much you will need to earn per hour for both the average private and public school. Not only does it affect the total amount of money you earn, but the more you earn per hour the more time you have to do other things such as studying. The dollars per hour amount you earn should be a conscious thought throughout everything you do when you work for yourself.

If you lose sight of how much you are charging, that dollars per hour amount will gradually decrease, meaning you will need to work more hours. *I used to calculate my revenue per hour every time I was finished with a job. Every single time. If my revenue per hour was lower than what I expected, I would try to figure out why it took me longer than expected so it didn't happen again.* {Sweet Tip} That dollars per hour amount was a motivator for me to improve my window cleaning efficiency.

So sit down with your parents and prepare the financial plan section of the

Gameplan. Remember, you won't know as a high school sophomore or junior whether you will get a scholarship or grant senior year. Use the national averages for now. And if you do end up getting a scholarship, fantastic! Take that as a bonus so you can work a little less that summer. Try to wrap your mind around the fact that you have a lot of work to do, and working toward making more per hour will make your goal that much easier to achieve.

Annual Cost of <u>Public</u> College: $22,000

Earnings $/hr	Hours of work required	# of 8-hr days required	Days you work a week	What this means:
$50	440	55	1	Work every day of summer break with one week off
$25	880	110	2.1	Work every day of summer break plus 5.5 days a month
$15	1,466	183	3.5	Work every day of summer break plus 13.6 days a month
$8	2,750	343	6.6	Work every day of summer break plus 31 days a month every day of the year

Public: Avg $20,000 + 10% = $22,000

Annual Cost of <u>Private</u> College: $40,700

Earnings $/hr	Hours of work required	# of 8-hr days required	Days you work a week	What this means:
$50	814	102	2	Work every day of summer break plus 4.6 days a month
$25	1,628	203	3.9	Work every day of summer break plus 16 days a month
$15	2,713	339	6.5	Work every day of summer break plus 31 days a month, (every day of the year)
$8	5,087	636	12.2	Work every day of summer break plus 64 days a month. (not possible)

Note: figuring a 12 week summer break (5 work days a week, M-F)

The advantage to starting in high school

Working for yourself during high school is an enormous advantage over waiting to do so until you reach college. Making the big bucks doesn't happen immediately. There is that ramp-up of training, learning, and figuring out how to do all this. There are no shortcuts. It's a progression to making more money per hour. That's why you start in high school, so that by the time you are in college you will be making the big bucks. During high school summer vacations, you can train and work as much as you can with no concerns about homework or classes, which may not be the case once you start college. This time enables you to learn your trade or skill, plus do a few side jobs. It might take you two to three years just to save enough money for that first year of college because, in the beginning, you are earning less than your dollars per hour goal. But even with the occasional party and road trip during summer vacation, you realistically have more than enough time to make your first year's tuition as well as expanding your knowledge so you can start making real money.

I learned in high school how to clean windows. By the time I attended college, I had four summers of window cleaning experience. On the expense side, by starting in high school you have relatively low expenses if any. You live at home rent free, maybe drive your Mom or Dad's car, and have all your daily expenses like food and electricity paid for. In other words: *High school is an ideal time for saving money.* {**Sweet Tip**} Start saving early enough and you will have the first year of college paid for before you set foot on campus. After those high school training and learning years your dollars per hour should be at a level where you can pay for the upcoming school year each summer.

We need to be clear that you won't be making $50 an hour right out of the gate. To be completely honest, you're going to be making significantly less when you start out. And to be even more honest, many of you will never reach $50 an hour. Some services just can't command such a rate. To earn $50 an hour you have to be exceptionally skilled and exceptionally efficient with a niche skill that customers are willing to pay that much for. So what happens if you can't get your earnings up to $50 an hour? What if you end up consistently making $25 instead? That is awesome! You are still making more than three times what anybody flipping burgers for $8 an hour makes. In addition you will gain knowledge of small-business practices that will prove beneficial for the rest of your life. You are not punching a clock. You are creating a system with your own skills to earn a well-deserved profit.

The truth is, anyone can do this; but not everyone is willing to do it and, again, most have no idea where to start. Many teens are just not willing to put in the time or the effort. I've heard it said this way: "Never follow your dreams. Follow your effort." It's not about what you can dream of. That's easy. It's about whether or not it's important enough to you to do the work required to be successful. That's why I say, "be the 10." Realistically only 10% are willing to exert the effort to do it. There are no shortcuts.

It takes training to become proficient, effective marketing to find customers, and a good work ethic to make it happen. It's not always fun, but is any job? It is, however, extremely rewarding. It may seem tough sometimes, but the feeling you get when you drive away from a four-hour job with $200 in your pocket is amazing. So is the sense of accomplishment when your customer tells you what a great job you did and when a customer's friend calls to hire you. It's the feeling you get when you understand which type of marketing works for you or when you design your first flyer or you pick up your first batch of business cards with your name on the front. These feelings far exceed the work involved. Do you feel this way when you punch out at your current job? I didn't think so.

Have fun and don't quit

With all of this talk about money, demographics, marketing, advertising, blah-blah-blah, and work-work-work, it can be easy to forget that this can be fun. It's an education, a challenge, and a good time all wrapped up in one big burrito the size of your head. If you find yourself taking this a bit too seriously, or anything too seriously for that matter, take a step back and look at the big picture. In fifty years do you want to look back and remember how much fun you had working for yourself, or do you want to look back and think, "Wow, I wasted so much time stressing."

I had fun working for myself. I really enjoyed most aspects of it. Hopefully you will feel the same way. I always found the feeling of independence to be quite empowering. There's nothing better than doing a job that you found, doing it your way, and doing it when you want to do it. This is you expressing your individualism and making a few bucks at the same time. To be honest there will be days when things aren't going quite right. Or maybe it really sucks doing the job from hell...and you will want to quit. There is always an easier road to take. I can tell you not to quit, but when that moment arises (and it will) just ask yourself, "When I am old, will I wish I had quit and failed or wish I had tried harder? Or did I trudge through the tough day and give it my all, learn from my mistakes, and become better at what I do? Did I work to achieve my goals and pay for college and learn the art of business, all the while making my customers happy?" That's something to be proud of. That is a good day at work.

Watch out for the reasons to quit – then do the right thing

1. It's too much work – Actually it's a lot of work. Work is work and an hour of work is an hour of work. I'd rather work hard and be compensated well for my efforts. If it's too much for you then practice this over and over, "Paper or plastic?"

2. I'm shy, I can't do that – Yeah, I know, most of you are shy. You are 17 and should be. Now get over it. You aren't a kid anymore. Go shake some one's hand and introduce yourself. It gets easier every time you do it.

3. I don't have a car – If you can't figure out how to get anywhere by way of transportation then it's just not going to work. Seriously. Get your pen out and sign those student loan papers.

4. I advertised and nobody's calling – Time to change your advertising. Change the approach. Study what is working for others. Stir the marketing pot, but stay focused and increase your marketing efforts.

5. I can't get the price I want – Okay, first, what's the market rate? Are you overpriced? Have you proven value to your customers? Are you looking in the right places? Can you add something of value with little expense? Is the timing off? (like seasonally)

6. I hate selling – Most people do. There is an element of selling involved in working for yourself. But don't use the word... selling. You're simply telling people about yourself and what you can do for them. You stand around talking to your friends all day, go talk to some customers too.

7. I can't get a training job – Keep trying. Have you talked to everyone that does that service? Did you offer to work for minimum wage? Were you prepared for the job interview? Could you try another service? I never knew window cleaning even existed before the day I picked up a squeegee as a summer job.

8. I'm afraid to give the customer a price – Giving your first customer estimate will give you butterflies in your stomach. Happens to everyone. Completely normal. With every estimate it gets easier. Be confident and just keep doing estimates.

9. Working for someone else is so much easier – Yep, it is.

10. This isn't fun – It's only as fun as you make it. With anything there are good days and bad days. Most of the time it has to do with attitude. I thought it was fun most of the time because I enjoyed what I was doing and what I was earning.

Above all else fear will make you want to quit. Fear is simply not knowing what to expect and not knowing how to handle it. It's like riding a bike. You want to ride the bike, but you are afraid of falling. You are afraid that your friends will see you fall. Both legitimate concerns. Then you try riding the bike and you do fall. What do you do next? Quit? Resign to walking forever? No, you get up and try it again and you don't fall. A week later you are riding around the block wondering why you were so concerned about falling in the first place. Think of it this way: most of the hard things that make you want to quit when you're working for yourself will also be issues on a job making $8 an hour working for someone else. So it's hard for $8, or it's hard for $25 or $50. You can enjoy your work for $8 or enjoy your work for $25 or $50. Your perspective is just that—yours.

What to expect when you start working for yourself

Year One – Training

The first year is all about the law of inverse proportion. While it's an obscure name, I can say that it does define your first four years of working for yourself. When you work for yourself you will find that in year one you will do a lot more work for a much lower financial return. However, by year four you won't have to work nearly as much for a significantly higher return.

At your age you may not realize that this is the way all business ventures work. The beginning is always the hardest part. There is more to do. You are not as familiar with the systems. You don't have many (or any) customers yet. You have literally no momentum. Therefore, when you sit down to fill out your Gameplan, you will see that the year one to-do list is far longer than year four's list. It's like building a house. There is a lot of groundwork in the beginning. You dig the hole for the basement, pour and waterproof the foundation walls, backfill, lay down your sill plate, and then you can start building your first wall.

This program is much the same way. During year one you need to start with a solid foundation. Your foundation is the knowledge you learn from training. *Training is not a step you can skip.* [**Sweet Tip**] This is where the 90 start to fall by the wayside because they don't want to invest in training time. Ironically they end up working for others and training a lot throughout their lives. You'll need to be properly trained by professionals for a minimum of three months in order to later charge the high dollars per hour we're going after. Training will give you the knowledge and practice you need.

Remember the old saying, "Practice makes perfect"? There's a lot of truth to that. Knowing *how to do something*, *being proficient*, and *being professional* can be far apart. Training shortens the gaps. So does self-educating, which is simply learning as much as you can about the profession or skill you choose. Training is the practice to make you perfect. To charge $50 an hour, you had better be good—professional good—at what you do. Learn all you can about every aspect of your chosen field. Ask questions, watch how the pros do it and imitate their movements, and practice the processes to increase your efficiency. Squeeze lemons faster; stir the lemonade perfectly. Watch how the pros deal with customers. Watch how they price jobs. Then, when you get home from working all day, do some research on the Internet. Get online and learn from forums, YouTube videos, you name it. Be the brightest, be the best, and believe me you will reap the benefits—financial and educational—of your acquired knowledge and persistence.

While you are training, look for side jobs. Side jobs are jobs unrelated to the skill you are training for. They are those odd jobs that no one wants to do, so people hire high school student to do them. I once had to remove an entire layer of corkboard from my aunt's living room wall. I don't know why it was there—must have been some nutty '70s fad. But it was glued on pretty well, and it took me an entire day to remove it—a good side job. I once got hired to chauffeur some businessmen to a seminar where they would be drinking, so they didn't have to worry about drinking and driving. Seek outside jobs and make sure the customers know you are available for such jobs. Clean out a garage for a neighbor, help someone move, clear brush, paint a house, trim bushes, babysit. Side jobs are opportunities to make money, and often they pay better than your training job. How you handle your side jobs is also part of your training. After all, you will be dealing with customers. This is a good time to figure out your strengths and weaknesses and what needs improvement. Keep in mind that life is all about learning, and this is just another learning experience.

 Go to the Training section of the Gameplan. There are many things for you to learn when you are training. Go through the list of questions I have provided, and make sure you can answer all of them. Please add additional questions and answers as well. This is a good place to keep all the information you are leaning from your training job so you can apply it when you start on your own.

Year Two – Working for yourself

Year two will be a bit different, and that will be exciting! Now it's time to start working for yourself. To begin you will use some of that hard-earned money from year one as start-up money. You want to be prepared for when customers start calling. You will need the proper tools, marketing materials, etc. Year two is the time you start applying all that you learned in year one as you start working for yourself. The challenges will be greater, but so are the rewards. By this point you should be filled to the brim with knowledge about your skill and consider yourself proficient in your field. At first only a few customers will come to your lemonade stand, and it will be stressful. Don't sweat it. Stay positive and keep marketing yourself. Just when you think it's never going to work, it will.

Once you have the first handful of customers and have treated them exceedingly well, they'll start spreading the word; and the line at the lemonade stand will get longer. During this phase it is crucial to stay focused and keep telling people who you are and what you do. At the beginning of year two, your dollars per hour will be quite low, yet higher than your training job. You will do some jobs here and there; but you will be spending most of your time marketing, which you can consider work time but not paid work time—thus the lower dollars per hour.

This is another point at which many will quit or fail. Marketing is absolutely necessary to find customers. Again, the law of inverse proportion applies. In year two you will do a lot of marketing for little return. However, effective marketing in year two will create business—and revenue—for you in years three and four. Don't forget about side jobs either. *Side jobs are important all the way through.* {Sweet Tip} Due to the random nature of side jobs you need to always keep your eyes peeled. I can't tell you how many side jobs I picked up from my window cleaning customers. It was like a game. How many customers can I find and how many jobs can I do for them? Have some fun with it. Year two is a great time to flash that Kid Card. Who wouldn't want to hire you?

Year Three – Working for yourself with confidence

Year three will be much, much easier than years one or two. In year three you will start seeing some serious financial return from all the marketing you did the previous year. And, unless you are completely booked for the summer ahead of time, keep marketing. Customers will move away or may not need you again this year, etc. Lots of things can happen, so keep up the marketing and pay close attention to what works and what doesn't. By year three you already know what you are doing, and you have improved your skills. You aren't getting butterflies around customers, and you are starting to enjoy the customers a bit more. You have a better grasp of what you are really capable of, and you start realizing which jobs fit you best. You are now doing jobs more efficiently, customers are referring you, and business is coming from all over. Year three is the year of momentum. You have some momentum from year two; you just need to keep it going.

Year Four – Squeezing lemons with maximum efficiency

At this point you are either a professional at your trade or very close to it. You have a very good grasp of how to conduct yourself, and there is always a long line at your lemonade stand. You are still marketing, but now you know exactly which marketing works and which doesn't. You have established yourself as a go-to person in your trade, and people do exactly that. They come to you because they know you are reliable and do good work. There's that Kid Card again, although at this point it's a misnomer. With what you have accomplished, no one sees you as a kid at all. You have built your reputation, and your dollars per hour are much higher than in the previous three years. In fact you should be achieving your dollars-per-hour goal on a consistent basis.

Remember inverse proportion? You are on the side of the pyramid you want to be on now, thanks to hard work in years one through three. It is all coming together at this point. Is there still work to do? Absolutely. Except this time, it's not so much like work. It's more like tweaking what you already do so well. You start perfecting your systems. You start maximizing your efficiency on the job. You market in a way that you know works. By year four you have proven that you have the will, the desire, the smarts, the work ethic, and the stamina to succeed. You approach customers now with much more confidence than back in year one. You are putting larger amounts into your college savings every day, and you should be damn proud of yourself. You are kickin' ass, taking names, having fun, and taking money to the bank...literally.

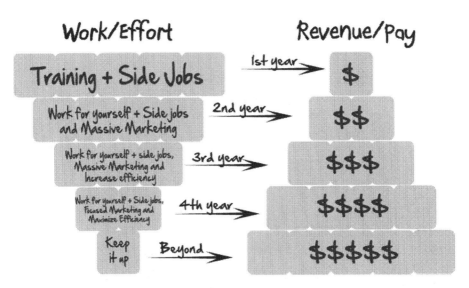

Time and money are interchangeable. You can always save one by spending more of the other.
–Roy H. Williams, *Wizard of Ads*

Time management and money management

Two things you can control and manage are money and time. The way you manage your money dictates the amount of free time you will have, and the way you manage your time dictates how much money you will have. They are interdependent. In high school your time is just that...*your* time. In high school you don't have the expenses that your parents do; they are paying your overhead. (This is a good time to go thank them!) You have free time regardless of your income. When you earn money in high school it is yours to save or spend.

Your parents are at a different point in their lives. How your parents manage their money dictates how much free time they will have...or if they ever get to retire. Your parents' main reason for working is because they have bills to pay. If they spend too much money, they have to spend more time working...and worrying. If they spend less than they earn, they will have more free time to do what they want to do. Why am I talking to you about how your parents manage money and time? Because working for yourself is all about managing your money (what you earn as well as what you spend) and your time (what you choose to do and not to do).

You've already learned from your parents about prioritizing, spending, saving, and working. That's the thing about being a parent: whether you intend to set an example or not, you always do. Your children are always watching. It's a blessing and a curse. Maybe you want to do things exactly the way your parents do; maybe you want to do the opposite or make some adjustments. Either way, really pay attention to what they do and how they spend. Maybe even talk to them about it. How much does your family spend on groceries every week? How much does it cost for heat in the winter? Do they have a budget that they follow closely, or do they wing it? How do they decide how much they can spend on Christmas presents or vacations? This knowledge will only help as you learn how to manage your money correctly, which, as you already know, will eventually affect your free time.

Free time...really isn't free

Just like you are going to earn your $88,000 for college bit by bit, you can spend your money bit by bit. Spend $5 here, $10 there; and then, at the end of the week, you are out of money and wonder where it went. "I never spent more than $5 or $10 anywhere," you might say. "How could I have spent it all?" It's the same with free time. It is so easy to procrastinate about things throughout the week. "I'll just do that assignment later," you tell yourself. "My friends are here, and I'm going to hang with them for a couple hours." or "I can flyer that neighborhood this week-end; I don't feel like doing it right now." Then all of a sudden the weekend comes, and you don't feel well due to the party you attended the night before that finished up at 3:00 a.m. You have assignments due Monday that you put off all week. You have to work the afternoon shift at your job. The next thing you know, you are not even considering working for yourself this weekend because all the short *free time* breaks you took the previous week added up and converged on the weekend. Just like your money, you should plan ahead where your free time will fit in or it will slip away from you. The clock keeps ticking regardless of what you are doing.

There are only 24 hours in a day, but there *are* 24 hours in a day—that's an enormous amount of time if spent/invested wisely. Everyone has the same amount of time. Your parents, your teachers, your manager at the low-paying job, Bill Gates—even the pope—all have those same 24 hours. *Carpe diem.* Seize the day. In those 24 hours, you have to fit in sleep, classes, a low-paying job, working for yourself, homework, projects/assignments, eating, transportation time, and of course free time and fun, which may or may not include doing nothing but just hanging out. Not that a person has to be productive all the time, but you'd be surprised how much time people spend doing nothing.

The problem is that college and high school students tend to prioritize fun and free time at the top, right below classes. So what do you really do with your time? *Write down what you do each day and the time spent doing it.* {**Sweet Tip**} The results will amaze you. Do you spend a lot of your time doing nothing? You can-not kill time without wounding eternity. What do you do with your twenty-four hours? Do you own the time or does the time own you? What if you changed your priorities? What if you prioritized earning and work above fun and hanging out with friends? What if you created a schedule that ensured you had time for both?

Again, I am not saying to work every minute of every day and not have any fun. On the contrary I say work very hard and efficiently when you do work so that you can make more dollars per hour, enabling you to have even more free time than the guy working for minimum wage. Making enough money to pay for your college years is important. Not only in regard to your education, but those college years can be the most fun you will ever have in your life.

If you live on campus, you have no parents telling you what to do, no cur-fews. Throw in a few road trips, parties, and Big Ten tailgates: does it get any better than that? But all this fun has a cost, which is time and cash. If you can work before college instead of during college you have solved the time-cash-fun issue all at once. One of my favorite quotes is, "The difference between being successful and unsuccessful is what you do with your time." That goes for work time as well as free time. Free time isn't really free; it comes at a cost. What are you giving up for that free time? Your schedule needs some flexibility, some play, but it needs structure, too. That structure mixed with a little discipline is how the 10 rolls.

Average hours per weekday spent by high school students in various activities

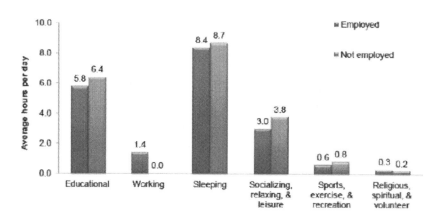

NOTE: Data include individuals ages 15 to 19 who were enrolled in high school. Data include non-holiday weekdays during the months of Jan.- May and Sept.- Dec. and are averages for 2006-10.

SOURCE: Bureau of Labor Statistics, American Time Use Survey

Time to optimize and prioritize

When researching for this book, I met with a young woman named Mary, who had worked a series of jobs in college to pay for college and graduated debt-free. (I love to hear that!) Like me, she had no financial help from her parents. If she wanted a college degree she needed to pay for it herself. She did everything from cleaning a meatpacking plant to bartending to tutoring student athletes. All those jobs paid between $7 and $15 an hour. She fit work around her class schedule so she could work as much as possible, because she had to. Mary worked on average fifty-six hours a week, took a full course load, and made the dean's list every single semester she was in college—quite impressive.

One thing Mary said really stuck with me. She said that she has friends who never worked during college, but they complain about working forty hours a week now after graduation. These people are complaining about working forty hours a week to a woman who worked fifty-six hours a week while taking a full class schedule as a college student. While the ability to work long hours may be a factor in your work ethic, it's probably not what you are looking to do freshman year (or any other year) in college. Mary did what she had to do to graduate with no debt.

Did Mary graduate with a fantastic work ethic? Yes! (It should be noted that she also graduated with a magna cum laude on her degree.) Would Mary's life have been easier if she had been making $50 an hour and could work less in college? Absolutely! When I asked her what she learned from the experience, she said, "Time management, without a doubt." She said she had to manage her time because there is only so much of it and she had to fit work and studies into each day. Mary also said, "I found that people who don't have to manage their time usually don't, and what I see as really small tasks seem to trip them up easily."

Time management is simply creating a schedule to optimize your time. Most likely you will want to optimize studying time during the school year and work time in the summer. Having a balance between work, classes, and fun is important and time management is how you accomplish that. So *break out a calendar, piece of paper, computer, or whatever and start prioritizing.* [Sweet Tip]

As a high school student, your school year is pretty well mapped out for you. That first summer when you are training will be scheduled by your employer. Try to schedule some weekends for side jobs when you are not training. Once you get to year two, things will change. You will be in sole control of your schedule, and the scheduling will become even more important.

Start by prioritizing your optimum times to work. If you are a window cleaner, you obviously want to schedule jobs during the day. Make sure your lemonade stand is open during peak thirst hours. When it comes to marketing yourself by putting out flyers, you may want to pick afternoons and weekends. If you are a pet sitter, you may want to schedule weekends for work. Since most people go away on weekends, that's when you will be busiest with pet-sitting duties. What your skill is and how it relates to scheduling will become evident while you are training. Also understand that things change, and any schedule will need to be adjusted at times.

Now let's talk about that summer break. The summer break is easy to schedule right? I mean, you have all day, every day to work. This is where I see teens get into trouble. It's easy to say in the summer, "I can stay out late because I can sleep in. I'll just work whenever I wake up." So you start getting up at 9:00 a.m. and starting work at 10:00 a.m. Then it gets a little later, and you start working at 11 a.m. every day. So what happened to those morning hours? They are now gone. Remember the relationship between money management and time management? You can look at it this way: Those two hours you slept in just cost you $100. Was it worth $100 to sleep in? Not a good deal in my mind.

It's a fact that many people are far more productive in the morning, especially if they are working outside and summer heat is an issue. Back to my favorite quote "The difference between being successful and unsuccessful is what you do with your time." What are you doing with your time? Are you using your time to make money, spend money, or sleep? A little self-discipline and scheduling will keep you on track. Pick a time each morning that you will start—regardless of how much sleep you got the night before. Pick, say, eight o'clock to be walking out the door each day. And if that's too early for you, then grow up.

There are a lot of high school and college students who arrive at work by seven o'clock every morning for their summer jobs. Sleeping in is a waste of time. And it's very common. Remember when we discussed that this program isn't easy? Remember the 10? The 10 get up in the morning and get things done. That is enough of the waking-up rant; let's get back to time management. The less time you waste, the more productive you are—period. Your time management skills will carry forward into your adult life and will prove to be crucial once you have graduated and start your career.

Money management

What's there to manage? You deposit the cash and you are done, right? Well, that's part of it. It's like your hair: it will just continue to grow. But if you don't clean, cut, and manage it once in a while, it will get out of control. Yeah, I know, you're not going to clean your money; but you will need to manage it. There are three aspects to managing money: earning, spending, and saving. I would go so far as to add a fourth: investing But we will save the Lemonade Stand Investing for another day. You know what these three terms mean; now let's see how this relates to your lemonade stand.

We aren't going to spend much time on the earning part here because, well, if you hadn't noticed that's what this book is about. I will say this, though: once you start earning, you'll probably be amazed at how easy it can be. Earning may well be where a lot of you need the most assistance getting started, but it's the spending and saving that will get you in the most trouble.

The biggest hindrance to paying for college, even if you do work for yourself, is spending your money wisely. You know what is smart and what is not when it comes to spending. But when you are faced with the possibility of purchasing something that you really want, do you have the discipline to say no? Can you do it? You will have the money, but it's earmarked for college. Maybe you can dip into your college savings just this once, just that one time. It's something you really, really want! And it's a super good deal! I know it's not easy, really not easy; it's downright hard to say no to yourself. Saving is discipline. Discipline is hard. Or is it?

It's really not hard if you have a plan and stick to it. Plan ahead of time where your money will go. Plan how much you will spend and plan how much you will save. For example, with every $100 you earn, take $75 and deposit it into your college savings account. You know the one. The one you never, ever, under any circumstances take money out of—yeah, that one. In other words, make a simple budget showing where the money will go. When you are in high school, you have relatively few if any monthly bills. Maybe you pay for your own cell phone or car insurance and probably for gas. So what we are talking about here is budgeting your college savings, spending money, and operating funds.

Operating funds? Where did that come from? If you are going to venture into the world of working for yourself, you will need to buy supplies along the way as well as start-up items. That lemonade stand will require the stand, a sign, cups, and some lemonade mix to start. Then after you sell out of lemonade, you will need to purchase more. You use your operating funds for that. With every dollar you earn, you will split it three ways. What percentage you save for each will be dependent on what your operating costs will be as well as your college funding goals.

Here is the best way to do it. If you haven't already, go open a bank account. Maybe you and your parents have already done this. If so, great, because you will need a place to put all this money you will be earning. You may want to start with a savings account. Or two savings accounts and a checking account. Why two savings accounts? Because it's very important to keep the money you save for college separate from any other money. Treat that college savings money like a one-way ticket. It can go one way (to the bank) but never return.

If you have trouble with this part (and some of you will), ask your parents to keep the college fund money in their names. That way there is absolutely no temptation because you know your parents will just say no when you beg them to access the funds. You will treat the operational funds differently. You don't want to keep them in a savings account. These funds must be accessible, sometimes on the fly. You need gas, you need squeegee rubbers, or your leaf blower just blew up—you never know when you will need these funds. Operating funds are best kept in a checking account, maybe with a debit card attached to it or a secured credit card.

So when is the best time to make bank deposits and start dividing funds? Immediately! Right away after getting paid. Right away. [Sweet Tip] Go directly to the bank, do not pass Go, do not collect $200. Go to the bank every day if you have to. Don't wait a week until you have $1,000 sitting there. Make your deposits daily. Why? I'll tell you why. Because you will spend the money otherwise.

That's what I did, and I regret it to this day. As a teenager who made some serious cash, I spent frivolously. I ate out all the time. I paid my friends' way into concerts and movies. I wasn't afraid to shell out the cash since I was making good money—$20 here, $50 there. It's hardly noticeable when you have $200 in your pocket after a job and you have more jobs scheduled tomorrow. Add all that up at the end of the summer, and suddenly that $50 bucks here and there is $1,000 or more—gone!

So be wise with your spending habits. They will carry forward into your adult life, and a little forethought and frugality will go a long way in terms of keeping your bank account on the positive side. Understanding finances now, especially your spending habits, will help you immensely down the road.

The convenience store is the enemy. Are you aware that the highest profit margins among retail food stores are at the gas stations? Candy bars cost more, soda costs more, even a pack of gum costs more than if you bought it at a grocery store. Why do they charge more? Because they can. People who walk into a gas station to buy a candy bar or a soda are buying on impulse, and they know that. Maybe you went there just to gas up and you are thirsty, so you go in and buy an energy drink. You just paid full-blown retail for that delicious refreshing pick-me-up. I know, I know, it's only fifty cents more than the same energy drink you buy at the grocery store, and what's fifty cents? That's nothing. And you are right. Fifty cents isn't much.

My first question is did you really need it anyway? Why didn't you pack a cooler of drinks in the morning? Drinks you bought at the grocery store or, better yet, your parents bought at the grocery store. I used to pack a cooler every day. Actually I still do. If you go to that gas station every day on your way to school and grab a donut and a drink and then go again after school to grab a snack, you just spent what? Maybe $5 to $10 each day at the gas station? Which adds up to $25 to $50 a week? If you are working part-time for $8 an hour, you have to work seven or eight hours just to pay for those gas station stops. My point is this: It doesn't seem like much when you pay $3 or $4 for snacks, but after time it adds up—much like the list of expenses after college. It's not that one can of Monster at a convenience store that will sink you. It's the culmination of stopping there every day that will make you go broke. (Sound familiar? It should. It's the same concept of bills in the debt cycle we discussed in chapter 2.)

Pack a lunch. {Sweet Tip} This habit will make a serious difference in your wallet by the end of the year. Again, one $7 value meal at the sandwich shop on the corner won't kill you. I know, you hate making a lunch in the morning and your mother hasn't done that for you since you were in sixth grade. Also that PB&J bag lunch isn't the most appealing thing to eat either compared to the latest foot-long special at the sub shop, but let's do the math. Spending $7 a day for five days is $35. Eating out for the whole school year would cost you more than $1,000. Packing a lunch is free when you live with your parents, and to be honest that packed lunch probably only cost your parents about $2.

I once worked with a guy once who would never, under any circumstances, eat out. He always packed a lunch. He felt that packing a lunch was healthier, and he didn't want to spend the money. He often said that once you get used to it you simply don't know any better. His discipline was commendable, and he had a fatter wallet for his effort.

Earning more than you spend = no financial stress

You will avoid years of financial stress if you earn more than you spend. Does it take discipline? Yes, quite a bit of discipline actually, but it gets easier the more you do it. It becomes a habit like brushing your teeth. It will require you to put off purchases until you save the money for them—in other words, delayed gratification. From my experience, learning these lessons at your age will benefit you greatly in the future. As I said before, college is an investment in yourself and in your future. So, technically, if you can pay for college without borrowing, you have effectively paid for your investment ahead of time. Flashback to high school econ class: an investment is an asset. An asset with no debt is a true asset. And a true asset is valuable. More valuable than you even realize.

Live within your means

My grandparents' generation never borrowed money except to buy a house or maybe a car, but nothing else. They would earn money, save it, and pay for things when they had the money to pay. They delayed their gratification. My parents' generation was introduced to debt when they became adults. They could get that car sooner if they borrowed the money. They could have an even nicer car if they borrowed just a little more and stretched the payments out another year. So they paid off the car in five years rather than four. For their entire adult lives, they were in debt.

My generation grew up in debt. We are all in debt. Some more than others. Debt is the norm. Everybody uses a credit card. Everybody owes on a vehicle loan (or two) and a home loan (mortgage). My generation lives in a world of instant gratification. Normal for my generation is being in debt up to your ears and working to pay the minimum payments. Hopefully your generation is different. Your generation is the smartest generation in history. I'm hoping that holds true for financial education as well. Without sound financial education, you are at risk of living in a world of debt like your parents.

What happens if you always earn more than you spend? What if you always pay for everything ahead of time? What if you never borrow a dime? What if you become the cheapest big earner around? What if you live within your means? Living within your means is a simple concept yet very hard to do. We live in a society where it's normal to take out a thirty-year mortgage on a house and a five-year loan on a used car. We buy furniture with zero down and free financing for two years. People use credit cards to buy groceries. We live in a culture where borrowing is the norm. Buy now and pay later.

But that's not what really happens. What really happens is that you buy things now and start a cycle of debt. This debt will surface every month in the form of a bill. Once you accumulate enough of these monthly debt bills, you are then spending most of your paycheck on them, the bills for things you already bought. Talk about stress! All the while you are eyeballing the next thing you are going to buy.

So what can you do? First, become educated on debt. Some of this education you can find right here in this book. Talk to your parents. I guarantee that most of your parents have felt debt stress at some point in their life, if not right now. Second, delay your purchasing gratification. If you can't pay for it in full now, then don't buy it. Force yourself to save up for it. Third, earn faster than you spend. I love this concept because it simplifies the equation down to its roots. You will never be in debt if you earn money faster than you spend it. Too often people will preach about "saving your money" and "don't go into debt," yet all they talk about is cutting expenses. But there are two sides to this equation. There is the earning side as well. If you can always earn faster than you spend, then you will never be in debt. Ever.

CHAPTER 4

Discovering your secret lemonade recipe

Patience is reading three chapters of necessary background information before
you get to the *how-to* part of the book.

—Geof White, hardworking but sometimes impatient author

What do you like to do?

So far we have been learning, training, crunching numbers, and planning. Now that
you've come this far it's time to make one of your biggest decisions: What kind of
lemonade stand are you going to open? Ask yourself the question, "What service can I
do that will provide enough dollars per hour to attain my financial goal of paying for
college?" While there is a whole chapter here of possible work-for-yourself services to
consider, there is no harm in providing an obvious service. Besides, let's remember that
your goal is not to start the next Microsoft empire…you need to do something with
low overhead and high revenue that will make you enough money to pay for college.
There is no need to reinvent the proverbial wheel. In this technology-driven, fast-
paced world we live in, people still need their lawns mowed, their leaves raked, and
their windows, bathrooms, and garages cleaned. They also need their children cared
for. In fact, the need for these common services is more abundant, so finding customers might be easier as well. Don't fall into the trap of being creative for creative sake.

The best place to start is to make a list of all the possible jobs you might enjoy or, at the very least, not really mind doing. Think about what your passion is.
Think about what you're good at. Think about something you do and people say,

"Wow! You did that fast!" or "That looks great!" Do you already have experience that you can draw from to jump-start ? You can also take the opposite approach and list what you don't want to do, which is equally valuable. You don't want to spend the next six summers doing something you hate.

I have provided a list of service-type jobs that are common among your age group. Most of these involve a low start-up cost and have the potential to make money consistently. Please go through the list and see what interests you, but remember that this is just a starting point, a launching pad. Keep brainstorming and add whatever comes to mind to the list. No matter how outrageous, get it on the Gameplan. Just spend some time writing and thinking. Ask your parents to help. After all, they have known you all your life. They may see potential in areas you are not thinking of. Possibly consider some of the searches you conduct on the Internet. If there is something that interests you enough to look it up online and spend hours reading about it, then surely it can hold your interest as work. Every lemonade stand is unique because everyone has a different idea of what a lemonade stand should look like. Every lemonade stand is also operated differently and, above all, everyone has her or his own super-secret lemonade recipe.

Another thing to keep in mind when making this list is that I'm generally referring to the numerous labor-intensive services a young person can offer. Service is the key term here. It's much easier to provide a service than to sell a product. I'm not saying you can't. I know a college student who brings in some serious money selling jewelry he makes himself from items he finds at antique and resale shops. This can be done, but I recommend staying away from doing something where you have to carry an inventory of products that need to be sold. The start-up costs of most services are fairly low because the product you are offering is labor, and your labor is free at this point. Carrying inventory is not. With inventory you immediately raise your start-up cost as well as having to deal with inventory in stock, slow shipping, items not being available when you need them, and a host of warranty issues you really don't need. Stick with your one product: labor. In addition services are best learned through hands-on experience, giving you ample opportunity to train. With services, you are selling yourself. You are your product.

The rest of this chapter deals with ideas and concepts that should be taken into consideration when choosing a job to do. So after you read through the list, be sure you finish the chapter before you make any decisions. Here is a list of services that meet some of our key requirements: service-oriented, training jobs easy to find, low start-up cost, plenty of demand, and recurring in many cases. Also many of these jobs can be done for the same customer as side jobs, minimizing your marketing costs. Keep in mind that this is a list I came up with. Your list may be totally different, and quite frankly I hope it is! Your list should be suited for you. This program is a little bit of economics and a whole lot of *you*.

Job List

Videographer

Website design

Mowing/gardening

Housesitting

Landscaping

Leaf raking

Computer repair/upgrade

Computer training

Graphic design

Musical instrument tutor

Foreign language tutor

Personal assistant

Bicycle repair

Garage/basement cleaning

Pressure washing

Gutter cleaning

Deck staining

Personal assistant

Childcare/nanny service

Window cleaner
(Oh come on! You didn't think I'd
forget that one, did you?????)

Fish tank cleaning

Flyer/coupon distributor

Smartphone trainer

Exercise class instructor

Pet sitter/dog walker

Editing/proofreading

Resume creation

House painting

Personal chef/meal preparation

Make and sell jewelry

House cleaning

Photographer

Snow shoveling

Blogging

Car detailer

Errand/courier service

Children's event/party planning

Holiday light installation

_____

_____

_____

After you pick your top possibilities for a service to provide, ask yourself the following questions:

- Would I like to do this?
- Can I keep busy doing this?
- Is there a need for this service in my area?
- Who would need it? Who is my target customer?
- Does this have low or high start-up costs?
- Is it a profitable service? How much can I charge?
- What is the frequency of service?
- Can I do this all year long or is it seasonal?
- Is it favorable for finding side jobs?
- Can I make money doing this?
- Do I understand the business cycles?
- Are there a lot of people offering this service?
- Is there a possibility of repeat customers?

Do for people what they *don't want* to do for themselves

Like no other time in history, people hire others to do all types of work for them. We live in a service economy. Americans have more money than any society in the history of the world, and what they are buying with it is *time*. Time has become the new currency. Your time is worth someone else's money. Someone pays you to do what you do best, and you pay someone else to do what he or she does best. It's your job to be the first one standing in line to say, "I can do that"—ideally before your potential customer ever asks for it to be done. Be willing to do the things that other people don't want to do. Think about it for a minute and see how many chores or tasks most people are capable of but don't want to spend the time doing. The first task that comes to my mind is cleaning. Most people do not like to clean or don't have the time to clean. People are capable of scrubbing the bathroom floor but just don't want to. That's where you come in. You tell them, "Hey, I'll clean your bathroom floor for $25 an hour. Shoot, I'll clean your whole house at $25 an hour." You may not completely enjoy cleaning, but all you have to do is crank up your iPod and away you go.

Landscaping, lawn mowing, snow shoveling, and painting are all tasks that most people are physically able to do but will hire out because they simply don't want to do them. Many adults value their time too much to do these tasks themselves. They find that the $40 they pay to get their lawn mowed is quite worth it because adults value their time and money differently than a high school student does. For example, $40 is worth more to a high school student than a doctor.

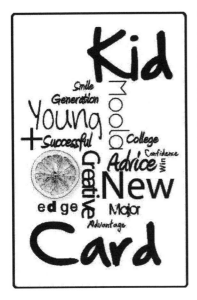

The time it takes to mow that lawn may be worth much more to the busy adult than the high school student, which benefits you now. Then, after you graduate from college and start making the big bucks, you can pay it forward by hiring a Kid Card-carrying high school student to mow your lawn, thus keeping the cycle of working for yourself alive.

When you finish this chapter, stop and make a list of all of the tasks people don't want to do. Let's see…pick up dog doo (eew), wash their car, mow their lawn, paint their house, wash their house, wash their dog, walk their dog…you get what I mean. Then compare it to the list you made of jobs you would be willing to do. Do any overlap?

Do for people what they *can't* do for themselves

Everyone can set up a lemonade stand, but not everyone can clean a window thirty-two feet high. People have limits as to what they can do, and you need to capitalize on that. We are all individuals with certain talents and skills. Use your skills to help others who are differently abled…and get over the word *capitalize*. This is a positive concept that gets negative press. There's nothing wrong with benefiting from someone's hiring you to do something she is unable to do. Everyone can't do everything. In the case of window cleaning, there are many reasons a customer can't clean her own windows (besides not wanting to). Perhaps the customer doesn't have a ladder tall enough, is afraid of heights, can't clean a window without leaving streaks, doesn't have the right tools, and has too many windows to finish the project in an entire weekend. Maybe the storm windows are too heavy for the customer to lift out. I can keep going…but I won't.

Some people simply don't have the ability or skills to do certain things. If something needs to get done, these people will hire someone to do it. Too bad he or she can't find a capable teenager with special skills to match the need. Kid Card time. Maybe you are a skilled musician. Many schools have cut their music programs, which means that if little Johnny wants to take tuba lessons he needs to take private lessons. I know a guy who has been teaching guitar lessons since he was in college and still does it fifteen years later because the money is so good. I have paid $25 an hour for my son to take drum lessons and $40 an hour for voice lessons.

Elderly people often fall into this *can't do for themselves* category. It can be a great opportunity, and you have the added satisfaction of helping out the older generation. Talk about a win–win situation. Now is the time when baby boomers are getting too old to take care of many routine tasks they used to be able to do. Baby boomers are people your grandparents' age and older. As World War II ended and everyone was so happy the Earth didn't blow up, they celebrated in a big way, resulting in a population explosion. The baby-boomer generation is larger than any previous generation, which makes for quite a few opportunities in the service world. So don't forget about the grandparent types. They're abundant, and many have disposable income. Disposable income means that they have extra money to spend. That is where you come in, with whatever service it is you're offering. As a bonus the elderly often live among others their age. Maybe if you do a good job, they will refer you to their friends. That Kid Card just keeps appearing, doesn't it?

Go to the Gameplan and list the jobs you want to do and don't want to do.

Specialty (niche) services

Every lemonade stand has the potential to make money, but some stands make more money than others. Maybe your lemonade tastes better. Maybe yours is the only lemonade stand in town. Maybe your stand is in a high-traffic area. Maybe you have a spotlight that reads "Cold Lemonade" against the cloud above. There are many possible reasons why you make more money than the kids operating other lemonade stands in town. But if you can find a niche, a specialty, you can almost guarantee that your stand will generate more money than others.

Window cleaning is considered a niche or specialty service in the cleaning world because it requires special skills and tools. What you can charge for window cleaning can be much greater—often double—than for, say, general house cleaning. People are far less willing to go out and buy tall ladders and specialty tools, then train to use them to clean their windows twice a year. In other words, they don't want to and often can't do it. It's quite common for niche skills to fit into both the *won't do* and *can't do* categories. However, the tools and chemicals to clean bathrooms and kitchens can be picked up at any grocery store. Anyone can do general house cleaning, but not everyone can clean windows. The frequency of demand for these two services will be different as well. Household cleaning may be needed once a week or once or twice monthly. Window cleaning jobs come maybe two or three times a year. The house cleaner may clean more frequently but usually for fewer dollars per hour than the window cleaner makes. Often the more frequent the service the lower the hourly pay.

Another good example illustrating this difference is tutoring as opposed to childcare. Tutoring is a specialty. Whether you are tutoring math, a foreign language, or a musical instrument, you will need a certain skill level to teach. This skill level may have taken years to attain, which translates into a higher per-hour charge. While childcare is just as important, it requires less specific knowledge or skill. The difference lies in the demand or need for the service. While a Spanish or violin tutor can charge $30 to $50 per hour, someone who provides childcare will have trouble attaining $15 per hour. The demand for childcare is much higher day-to-day than it is for tutors, but the supply of babysitters is even greater.

While specialty services might command a higher price, there might not be as many opportunities out there. Or are there? A Spanish tutor may only be needed once a week, while many, many parents need childcare daily. Personally I prefer to go with a higher-dollar niche service and then go out and find more opportunities. I have never had trouble finding people who want their windows cleaned. Or should I say, I have never had trouble finding people who want to pay my price to have their windows cleaned?

Of course window cleaners have other factors like weather and the economy to deal with, but in general they just need to find good customers. Every house has windows that could be cleaned, but not every house has a dog to walk or a bilingual child to tutor. I have always been willing to search for customers in need. If you can find those customers and work as many hours cleaning windows as your friend does cleaning houses, then you will be making more money. If you do happen to clean houses, don't let the window cleaner bug you. You're still making substantially more than the fast food or retail industry is paying. Niche services are at the top of the service pay scale, and it's obviously worth looking into services in this category.

Demand, frequency, and repeat customers

Making money offering a service is dependent on several factors that may be out of your control. Or can those same factors be used to your advantage? No matter how much passion, attitude, or time you throw at your new venture, there will be things that limit your work at times. Things like business cycles, which are sometimes called market timing.

Every service has a business cycle, which is driven by demand. A business cycle is simply a flow of demand—sometimes high, sometimes low. The residential window cleaning cycle in the northern states sees enormous demand in spring and fall, while demand is slightly less in the summer and almost nonexistent in winter. Obviously this cycle is driven by weather, which can be a major factor to deal with if you are working outdoor jobs.

On the other hand, that weather can create demand for other services. Who says the window cleaner who is slow in the winter can't pick up a shovel and start shoveling snow all winter until the spring window cleaning season? Your training should give you a better idea of what drives the demand, whether it is a certain part of town, a certain time of year, a certain age group, or any other demographic. It is up to you to find the demand and take advantage of it.

Business cycles will also drive the frequency of service. These factors all work together. A lawn mowing business cycle in the northern states starts in the spring and ends in the fall. Depending on how much it rains, those lawns may need to be mowed once a week, every three days, or in the heat of the summer every other week. From your training you should know what your business cycle will be. You will find tutoring more prevalent during the school year. There is a huge spike in all cleaning services during spring cleaning season. This is also good information as it relates to marketing for more opportunities, which we will discuss in the next chapter.

Once you have a good handle on how your skill fits into a business cycle, you can start to cultivate repeat customers. Those repeat customers are what keeps the cash coming in. Constantly going out and finding new customers is costly and time-consuming. For every new customer, there is the time spent advertising, bidding, describing your service, explaining what you will and won't do, —and that's just to prepare for the first job.

Repeat customers already know what you do. You have met or exceeded their expectations previously, and they feel comfortable enough to have you back again on a regular schedule. Maybe you are scheduled to mow the lawn the same day every week. Just show up, do your job, get paid, and go home. Sounds a lot like an employee punching in and punching out, doesn't it? Except *you* keep the profit. Repeat customers who are treated right will have a positive long-term effect on your business. *By doing a service repeatedly for the same customer, you will naturally get more efficient doing that job.* {**Sweet Tip**} If you price the job right, your increased efficiency will increase your dollars per hour simply because you will finish the job faster. That repeat customer will most likely appreciate your work; otherwise he or she wouldn't have you back. The level of trust and confidence will grow over time, and that repeat customer will be your best bet for referrals as well as side jobs. Anyone who is happy with your work will be happy to refer you to friends.

Think of it this way: the job is not complete until the customer is so happy that he confidently makes referrals. Play that Kid Card—everyone wants to see you pay for college, right?

Side jobs

You have already started developing ideas about what you can do to work for yourself. This would be your main skill and the service that will get your foot in the door with customers. This skill will provide most of your money and be the main reason you establish a relationship with the customer. You will, however, find opportunities to make some extra cash here and there if you keep your eyes and ears open. There will be times when you don't have enough window cleaning jobs or times when you see another chance to help a customer out. Be proactive. Ask the customer if she needs some help.

Side jobs are extra services you offer to your customers but don't advertise. Often these are unexpected jobs generated by the customer's needing something done and turning to you to solve the problem. Keep in mind, too, that whatever need you fill or demand you satisfy, there will always be related yet different side jobs that you can add on. Heck, you may end up doing something totally different from what you initially intended to do. I could have very easily ended up painting every day instead of cleaning windows. Painting jobs just kept presenting themselves to me. Once a person has hired you to do one task, the chances are pretty high that he'll eventually say, "By the way, is there any way you could do this other thing for me?" It's easy for a customer once he trusts you, and he wants to help you pay for school.

Say your window cleaning customer has some limbs hanging over her gutters and her bushes are a bit too overgrown. . .what's that. . .a side job opportunity? Don't be afraid to mention to a customer that you can help in other areas if you feel those areas need attention. Play the Kid Card. Be straight with her. Tell her you are looking to pay for college and you'd appreciate some extra work. Just remember to be tactful, and don't insult the customer.

You don't want to say, for example, "Those bushes in front of your house look horrible. I can trim 'em up for ya if ya pay me extra!" Be a little smoother and say something like, "I noticed the shrubs around the front are a little overgrown. If you'd like me to come over some time to trim them back a bit, I'd be happy to do that." *If you get enough side jobs, you could say you are side-jobbing your way through school.* {Sweet Tip} Once customers find out that you are a hardworking, dependable, and trustworthy student, they will find more jobs for you to do. So sometimes and eventually more often, you won't even have to inquire about a side job with the customer; the customer will just ask you.

People hire people they trust

Side jobs can be so lucrative and abundant because of one word: trust. Well, maybe two words: trust and comfort. Here's an example. If you get two service estimates to repair your car, one from a stranger and one from a person you're familiar with, who are you likely to go with? Let's take this one step further. The first quote is a bit lower, but you don't know the mechanic and aren't familiar with the quality of his work. The other quote is presented by someone you've met before, you've heard good things about, and you're somewhat comfortable with. Most people will pay the extra money to have the work done by someone they trust and/or are comfortable with.

After you establish that you are punctual, hardworking, and get the job done right the first time, your customer will be impressed enough to hire you for other tasks, not to mention referring you to friends. Another benefit of establishing trust with your customers is that they don't question prices quite as much. They're happy to have quality work done for a reasonable price, and they feel good that they're helping a college student pay for school. Everyone loves the college kid— another Kid Card sighting.

Some of the side jobs I picked up from window cleaning back in the day included painting houses, painting windows, staining decks, landscaping, removing old carpeting, helping people move, cleaning out garages and basements, fixing roofs, and even car detailing. My neighbor used to pay me $30 to detail his car every week. It would take about an hour, so I benefited from good frequency and good per-hour pay.

Seasonal jobs

In addition to side jobs, there are seasonal jobs that can only be done at certain times of the year. There are short seasons and long ones. Back in New York, most customers only want their windows cleaned in the spring, summer, or fall, whereas in the South customers want their windows cleaned throughout the year. Raking leaves, shoveling snow, and installing holiday lights are all short-term seasonal jobs. What I like about the seasonal jobs is that people are apt to hire them out. These seasonal jobs are considered a pain in the butt by most customers and can provide much-needed income in a short period of time for a motivated student.

Have you ever helped your parents hang holiday lights on your house before the holidays? Well, guess what? People are willing to pay big bucks to have that done. And if you are the window cleaner who happens to have ladders, then you are already set up to do it. I have had customers pay me more than $1,000 to hang Christmas lights and wreaths and to put out the lighted holiday figures. The best part is you will need to take them down as well. It's an opportunity that presents itself right around Thanksgiving and again right after the holidays are over. So you can make some quick cash to buy gifts, and then you can make a little more cash right after the holiday because you overspent during your school break. I can't be the only one who tends to overspend during the holidays.

One last thing…

I must emphasize how important it is to find something you like to do. There is nothing worse than spending eight (or more!) hours a day doing something that drives you crazy, when doing something you like can be fantastic. The time seems to go by faster, and you will be more satisfied with your accomplishments. That difference between hating what you do and liking what you do can also have a major effect on your attitude outside of work. I mean, we all have the friend who constantly complains about his job, right? So what happens if you pick a service and you later decide that it just isn't for you? Well, that's the beauty of being a teenager—actually the beauty of life—because you can always change gears and move in a different direction, although it may require some additional training.

Maybe you picked a service that is similar to other services and you like one of those other services better. I was a window cleaner, but I did a lot of painting, too. I could very well have become a painter instead of a window cleaner. It's not a bad idea to consider complementary services when you choose your training job. Akin to side jobs, complementary services are those that enhance or are done in conjunction with certain other services. Window cleaning works well with pressure washing as well as gutter cleaning. If you can find a group of services to do, it will afford you the variety of not doing the exact same thing every day. Often when someone does the same thing every day, it's not the job itself but the lack of variety that makes it difficult.

All of this boils down to the simple concept of having some forethought and being informed before making a decision as to what service to choose. Choosing a service can have many variables. Hopefully there is enough information here for you to start the process of matching your personality and skills with a profitable service. Get your parents involved. They know your personality and capabilities better than anyone. After all, they helped you with your first lemonade stand. And no one wants to see you succeed, be happy, and pay for college more than your parents!

CHAPTER 5

Recognizing thirsty people and offering them a drink

Thomas Edison is credited with saying, "Most people don't recognize opportunity because it's usually dressed in overalls and looks a lot like work."

Hey! Did I just see an opportunity over there? Opportunities are everywhere.

Your lemonade stand is built and it's time to put out the *open for business* sign. Maybe customers will come, but most likely at first you will need to go find them. Or at least let potential customers know where your lemonade stand is and what you are serving. You need some good old-fashioned marketing to create opportunities. You see, opportunities need two parties to work successfully: the person offering or providing the opportunity and the person who seizes the opportunity.

You are the one holding up your Kid Card saying, "I'm ready to seize an opportunity." You just need to find the people willing to give you the opportunity. They are out there. People want and need lemonade. You just need to find them and direct them to your stand. Your services as well any side jobs are all a product of recognizing and taking action when you see an opportunity. So what does an opportunity look like? What should you look for?

The best way to recognize an opportunity is to first know what you are capable of. Then keep your eyes and ears open while you market yourself and your service. Look for places where your service is needed. Look in your neighborhood; have your parents look at work. You will often discover opportunities while working for another customer. Customers will mention things that turn into opportunities. Say I'm scheduling a window cleaning and the customer says, "I'd really like to have my windows cleaned before June 16th because we are having a wedding reception in our back yard that day." You reply, "I will come on the 14th at 8 a.m. to clean your windows. Would you like any help setting up for the reception?" What? Are you catering now as a side job? Nope, but it's still an opportunity.

True story. A lady hired me to clean the windows and also hired me to come the day before the reception just to help set up. I was the gopher. I hauled what seemed like 4,000 chairs and tables that day. I moved lawn furniture around and even cleaned out the pool—all the jobs she didn't want to do and didn't have time to do before the wedding— but I was glad to do them! I was there all day and she paid me a couple hundred bucks, not to mention fed me lunch. It was kind of fun, but not something I would have anticipated or advertised on my flyer. I also picked up another window cleaning job when one of the woman's relatives stopped by that day. Seek opportunities; they are literally everywhere. You just need to get good at recognizing them.

Know your capabilities and know where to look. It's like fishing. If the fish are biting by the shore, fish by the shore. Use your Kid Card as bait, and fish where the customers are.

An opportunity disguised as an old water heater

When I moved into my current home, the previous owners had left an old broken water heater in the basement. My nephew and I hauled that heavy beast upstairs to put out on the curb. All I had to do was buy a $10 tag and leave it out there for the local municipality to pick up. We got as far as the garage when I hear "Hey, you gettin' rid of that?" I look over and it's the high school neighbor kid Austin. I say "Yep" and he runs over, grabs the dolly with the water heater on it and says "I'll get rid of it for you" and throws it in the back of his truck, brings back the dolly and says "Thanks! I'll take it to the recycler." Cool. I don't have to stop and buy that $10 tag now. I don't even have to walk it to the curb. But wait, it gets better. His dad walks over and says, "He's been taking a lot of stuff to the recycler lately. His school got all new computers so he went to the principal and said "Would you mind if I took all the old computers to recycle them?" The principal said "Sure, now I don't have to worry about disposing of them." What he was doing was taking all the metal insides out of the computers and taking them to the recycler and getting paid scrap prices. According to his dad he had made a couple hundred bucks already bringing in scrap metal. When the neighbor kid saw me hauling that old water heater to the curb he saw an opportunity. He was aware of his capability and seized the moment. Entrepreneurial spirit at its best!

Let's go find some customers, aka opportunities

All that you've learned thus far is rendered useless without customers, right? You also know that the beginning is the hardest part; this holds true with any endeavor you embark upon. Riding a bike, playing a sport, and finding customers all become easier the more you do them. The fact is that the beginning can be so overwhelming and so intimidating that most people with a good idea never pursue it. Every person has a million-dollar idea at some point in his or her life, but very few take action. If you take a deep breath and actually start, you are already well ahead of the rest.

So now you are working for yourself. Where do you start to find customers? Will someone actually hire you? What advertising works? What's the difference between advertising and marketing? How much is it going to cost? How much can you make? What if people don't hire you? And the list goes on... I can hear some of you now: "Ah, screw it! Where's my apron and hat? I'm going back to work at the sandwich shop." Wait a minute! It's another *be the 10* moment. Time to prove why you are the 10.

All of these are normal, legitimate concerns disguised as questions. Anyone who works for him- or herself had the same questions in the beginning. You will find that, once you start, it's really not as hard as you think. After finding your first few customers, your confidence will grow and finding more customers will get much easier. I felt exhilarated when I found a new customer. I enjoyed the process: the introduction, showing up to the job the first time, doing a good job. I love seeing the smile on the customer's face while she hands me a check and says, "My windows look fantastic, and I will tell my friends about you." It's more than just making good money. The sense of accomplishment when satisfying a new customer really feels good. But before we get into ways to market yourself, let's look at the biggest hurdle for most high school students.

Overcoming fear and rejection

What if the customer says, "No, thanks"? It will happen. And...well...it's character-building time. Keep in mind that how you react to rejection can affect future business. You may actually impress the customer with a mature response to rejection. The customer may refer you after that or even change her mind and hire you in the future. First, let's deal with the aspect of rejection. Rejection can (and will) cause negative feelings. Your face might turn red, you might feel a knot in your stomach, you might get mad or even sad. These are all normal feelings; don't let them overwhelm you. Maybe you've heard the phrase, "Salesmen have thick skin." What that means is salesmen don't sweat being rejected. In fact, a typical professional salesman's spin on that is, "If you are not getting rejections all the time, you're not trying hard enough." To them rejection is just part of the job. So be prepared because you will face rejection at some point. But, just like finding customers, dealing with rejection gets easier over time.

Here's a perfect example of what rejection can be like. A few years out of college, I had a customer who actually swore at me and threw me off his property when I gave him an estimate. He wasn't mad at me; he was mad at the price. He had in his head that it was going to cost X and the actual price was X plus quite a few dollars. After he yelled at me, I quietly left. He called me and had calmed down by the next day, so I went back and he was apologetic. He signed the order, and our interactions were smooth for the remainder of our relationship. People reject for a number of reasons. Notice I said people *reject*, not people *reject you*. Usually it's not personal, unless you showed up to the estimate dressed like a homeless person, with your cell phone ringing off the hook while you were swearing and spitting the whole time. Then maybe it was personal. You will be surprised how few people will actually say no if your price is fair and you do a good job of presenting yourself. Play that Kid Card, and everything will be fine.

So when the customer does say no, what do you do? First, be professional and don't show any hint of being upset. (This is hard to do, but it shows a lot of maturity.) Maybe you could play off your internal upset with a little humor, but realize that nobody wants to say no to a teenager—more likely the person wants to say yes. When people say yes to someone, it produces a good feeling inside while a no creates the opposite feeling. In all circumstances of rejection and whether you employ humor or not, put out your hand, thank the potential customer for the opportunity, and say, "May I ask why you said no?" Here's another opportunity to play the Kid Card. "I want the fact that you said no to be a learning experience for me; would you care to elaborate on why you said no?" This noncustomer will immediately start thinking that you are a mature young adult. Is this a hard question to ask? You bet! But this is a fantastic learning opportunity. That person may say, "Your price is too high" or "I don't think you will finish in time" or "Maybe next year" or "I'm just going to do it myself" or "Those times don't work for me" or "I can't afford it right now." All legitimate reasons not to hire you.

Once you find out what the objection is, you may be able to save the deal or at least learn from this rejection so you can try to avoid it next time. The person may not be forthcoming after you ask that question, but don't push it. On the other hand, the person may state a problem that is easily remedied. All of this will help you in the future. Or, heck, perhaps, after hearing your question, the person says,

"You know what, maybe I'll give you a shot." After any rejection I would also follow up with a card in the mail that says, "Thank you for the opportunity. If you know anyone else who can use my service, please pass along my business card." Yes, even after rejection, you should ask for a referral because referrals are the most powerful form of marketing you can employ. (We'll get to that later.)

Managing the fear

This is not a program for the faint of heart. You may find a lot of this terrifying, or maybe it raises your blood pressure a bit. Regardless of your age, you will get butterflies in your stomach when you walk up to that first customer's house. Don't worry. After you have done it for a while, those butterflies will turn into excitement. At seventeen it can be hard to walk up to someone's house, introduce yourself, shake a stranger's hand, and proceed to give him a price on a job. It's not necessarily overcoming the fear; it's managing the fear and not allowing it to overcome you. There are certain traits most successful people have in common regardless of business, industry, occupation, gender, or time in history. One of those traits is managing fear.

Fear of meeting new people is very real to some people. It's not just young people who have this fear either; many adults have this same fear. This fear has kept plenty of adults in jobs where they don't have to shake hands or make eye contact with others but simply work by themselves. I believe you need to beat that fear into submission at some point in your life, so why not now? I say the earlier the better.

So how are you going to get over this fear? Here are some practical suggestions to help you with shyness and fear. Nothing changes completely overnight, especially an issue that has most likely been around your entire life; so don't be frustrated when you aren't suddenly acting like a politician and kissing every baby you see. Patience and determination are key to handling this. You can do it; it just takes practice. You can start by practicing greeting people. Fake the confidence if you have to—fake it 'til you make it. Pretend it doesn't bother you. Pretend it's easy. Start with people you know or your parents know.

Maybe your mom or dad can take you to work and introduce you around under the guise of Take a Kid to Work Day. The coworkers or employees won't know you're working on shyness and will be pleased to meet you, so there is absolutely no rejection involved. They might be people you have met before or not, but instead of acting like a kid and saying "Hi" shyly while staring at the floor when you are introduced, act like a young adult and give each a good handshake. Make eye contact and say, "Nice to meet you." You might have to force yourself to do it at first. But the more you do it, the more comfortable and confident you will become. Get in the rhythm of that handshake and that "nice to meet you." This may seem like it's all becoming a bit ridiculous and it may very well be; but, hey, who wants to be less than completely prepared? Keep shaking hands and introducing yourself until it becomes natural; repetition and practice are key.

The same principle applies to any task you try to accomplish. If the motions are natural, even if you are meeting someone new, no one will be the wiser that you have an issue with being shy. One thing to remember that might give you a little peace of mind is that most customers will be glad to see you. After all, they did call you for an estimate or to hire you. When a customer is glad to see you, everything should be just fine. You will go through your introduction and discuss what needs to be done.

Fake it 'til you make it

I have a nephew who lives with us in the summers. When he was seventeen he worked for me and became proficient at cleaning windows. When he moved back home his plan was to make some money his senior year of high school cleaning windows. We made up some really cool flyers to post and give to neighbors. He did one job for a friend's mother but that is where it ended. The job wasn't too hard and he made a pretty decent hourly rate. The reason he didn't proceed and put out more flyers is that he was too shy. He was afraid to talk to customers and instead of facing and conquering his shyness and fear he chose to turn the other way.

Maybe you're not the most confident person in the world, or maybe you're just not very confident when speaking to adults. That old cliché, 'fake it 'til you make it' comes to mind right now. Meaning even if you aren't comfortable at something just act like you are comfortable with it (fake it) until you are comfortable doing it (make it).

As it turns out, my nephew did get over his fear. It was about a year later when he started college but he didn't clean windows this time. Cleaning windows really wasn't his thing. He started working for himself as a professional organizer and that fear of rejection and shyness went away almost immediately. He felt comfortable talking to people about organizing whereas he was uncomfortable talking to customers about window cleaning. He found his niche, overcame the fear and away he went.

Marketing for opportunities

Now before you run out the door in search of your first customer, we need to cover some basics. There are many ways to acquire customers, most of which require marketing. Let's get some marketing definitions out there so you can gain a better grasp on the information relating to finding good customers. Keep in mind when it comes to finding customers that it's a process of utilizing all of the following tricks, not just one or two. They overlap. They feed off each other, and once that process is rolling your phone will ring. The term for this is circular momentum (see below). You may already know these terms, but let's take a look at what they mean to you in this specific situation. Once you're finished with this chapter, chances are that you'll have a better understanding of small-business marketing than most adults you know.

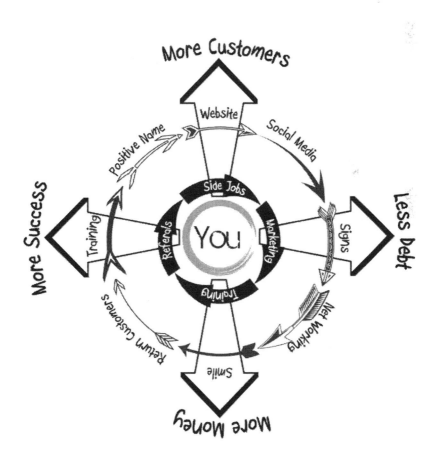

Marketing

This is the activity and processes for creating, communicating, and delivering offerings that have value to customers. Marketing is more of an overall approach taken to gain business, whereas advertising and networking are components of marketing.

What it means to you

Marketing is the broadest term that includes all forms of advertising, sales, and contact with potential customers. Think of marketing as the umbrella, and all the various forms of customer contact are under the umbrella. Your marketing strategy will involve advertising, networking, sales, and any form of getting the word out to potential customers that tells them who you are and what service you offer. The more people who know what you do, the more your phone will ring.

Your marketing plan

Everyone needs to know you have the best damn lemonade in town. Jobs are not going to fall into your lap. Well, a few will, but not enough to fill up the summer schedule and definitely not enough to pay for college. I completely understand that it can be hard to get motivated to go out there and market yourself. It seems like there are always other things to do than marketing; you've got friends, girlfriends, boyfriends, parties, homework. You will need some discipline because marketing is essential to your success. So *schedule yourself to market yourself.* {**Sweet Tip**} Budget your marketing time like you budget your money. Make marketing yourself a priority because, until you have enough paying customers, marketing yourself is your job. Don't be afraid to get creative and have a little fun with it, too.

In the beginning it will seem as if you are marketing like crazy for just a job here and there. Fast-forward six years and you will hardly be marketing at all, your summer booked solid. (Remember inverse proportion?) Be efficient and smart when marketing. This saves on marketing expenses. Your best bet is to use multiple forms of marketing with an emphasis on lower-cost forms, namely referrals. I know, who is going to refer you if you don't have any customers yet?

Again, starting is the hardest part. This is where flyers, Facebook, and networking become important. Bombard the neighborhoods with flyers on nice sunny days. Market specifically to a certain demographic that is most likely in need of your service. At night work on your Facebook page and your website. Look for free networking events sponsored by a chamber of commerce or local business groups. Make a point to hand business cards out at the hair salon around the corner. Give your parents flyers to put up at work. I used to say to myself before I'd go flyering, "I'm going to find some work today." A positive attitude will make this whole process a lot easier if not kind of fun. If nothing else, walking a neighborhood flyering is great exercise!

Marketing materials

So what does this flyer need to say? What should your business card look like? How big should the sign be? With any marketing piece, start out by thinking like your customer. What does the customer want to see and hear? What do you want the customer to know about you and your service? Make sure you include the Kid Card and your willingness to do side jobs on everything you use to market yourself. Those two concepts alone will bring in new customers.

Market the Kid Card

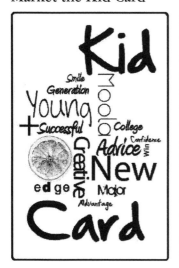

Customers will be drawn to the fact that you're working to pay for college, so use it in your marketing. It's quite admirable and you should be proud of it. Saying you are working to pay your way through college is a marketing advantage, and any advantage is better than no advantage. Adults like to hire the hard-working college-bound student, but they may not know what you are doing. So it's up to you let them know what you are doing and why.

Advertising

This is a form of communication intended to persuade an audience to purchase or take some action upon products, services, or ideas.

What it means to you

Advertising is simply letting people know who you are and what you do in whatever form you choose: signs, business cards, a magnetic sign on your car, flyers, anything that promotes you. If you are a window cleaner, your advertising should say "Window Cleaning" or better yet "WINDOW CLEANING," as well as what type of window cleaning you do. My flyers used to say, "Residential Window Cleaning – Call Geof White – Free estimate" with my phone number. If I were doing it now, I would add my website and Facebook page.

Keep your advertising eye-catching and fun. Put some thought into layout and design of your advertising, even if it's done on your home computer. Think about prominent images for your flyer as well as color choice. Contact information should be on all advertising. Avoid any kind of harsh language, unless of course your business is selling bumper stickers that specialize in creative use of the f-word. In that case…bombs away. The more involved you are with every aspect of your advertising, the more pride you will have when customers call. And to tell you the truth, it's pretty satisfying to take your own photos, write your own words, put them all together in a decent layout, and be able to tell people, "This is who I am and this is what I do."

What should your advertising say?

Again, think like the customer for a moment. Think about what message a potential customer wants to see on your advertising in order to make the decision to call you. What problem can you solve for him? How can you help her out? Your most likely customer may live next door; but if the neighbor doesn't see something that says you clean windows, how will he or she ever know? Advertising should always have contact information as well as the obvious what-you-do message. Think about what advertising you see every day. Is there a certain style or technique that looks better to you than others? Maybe you will decide to go classy with your message or maybe bold, cute, or sassy. Whatever you choose make sure it's simple enough for the customer to understand the message you are trying to get across.

Good old-fashioned yard signs

This is a simple concept and probably the oldest form of advertising. After all, the customer will see your sign and then call you, right? Maybe. Signs are not always as effective as referrals, flyers, or networking; but signs are definitely worth the effort and relatively low cost. I'm not talking about a billboard on the highway. I'm talking about one of those signs you see in people's front yards, the type that politicians use when running for office or contractors use while they're on a job.

Those signs can be made relatively inexpensively ($20 to $30) online or at the local sign shop. If I planned on spending at least half a day cleaning windows at someone's home, I would put a sign out—with the customer's permission of course—so the neighbors would know who was doing the work.. It might also be a good idea to put a sign in your own front yard if your neighborhood allows that kind of sign. You could also purchase magnetic signs for your car or truck, and now your vehicle becomes a mobile sign.

So what should your sign say? If we are taking yard signs, you need to keep it simple. People can only retain so much information as they drive by and catch a sign out of the corner of their eye. My yard signs were simple. They read, "Window Cleaning – Free estimates" with my phone number. Three lines for the customer to see. Very simple. I used a blue background with contrasting large yellow lettering. Easily read from the road. Sometimes I would leave a sign out for the day and sometimes for the week. Your customer will tell you what he or she is comfortable with.

Referrals

A referral occurs when one person recommends or endorses a qualified professional or service to another person.

What this means to you: Referrals are king. They're the lowest-priced and best form of marketing there is. You want to make money and make your life easier? Ask for referrals, ask for referrals, and ask for referrals. Did I say that three times? Hmm, I wonder why. Yes, it's that important.

People who are happy with your work will be happy to refer you to others, which just so happens to be networking as well. See the overlap? Remember how customers hire people they trust? When someone refers you to a friend, the trust is incorporated in the referral. If I trust Bob and Bob says that an ambitious young high school student did a fantastic job painting his house, I'm likely to trust that student right out of the gate because I trust Bob. Reputation is everything when it comes to referrals. If you have a reputation as a good-natured and hardworking teenager, you have it made. Referrals will reproduce like bunnies. If you have the reputation as a teen who cuts corners, shows up late, and doesn't finish the job... well, good luck!

Here's an idea: *Make it easier for people to refer you.* [**Sweet Tip**] Get business cards and hand them out to your customers so they can give them to their friends and neighbors, thus assisting the referral process. Leave business cards as if you were leaving a popcorn trail to get back out of the woods. Order a couple hundred business cards, and make sure they look awesome. Design your card with all your info on the front of the card. List your services on the back. Or the back might simply read, "I want to graduate from college with no debt so I am working for myself." Then, when you finish cleaning windows at Betty's house, give her four business cards. Ask her to keep one and give the rest to her friends. And when Wilma calls and books you for next week, you will see the power of a referral. It takes you about one minute to hand someone a business card and ask for a referral. If the recipient of just one card calls, then it worked. It bears repeating: A referral is the best, easiest, most cost-effective marketing strategy there is. Play the Kid Card, ask for referrals, and listen for the phone to ring.

Networking

This is the cultivation of productive relationships for employment or business, utilizing the exchange of information or services among individuals, groups, or institutions

What it means to you: Networking is like a web. It means interacting with people who may need your service or may recommend your service to others. Sometimes networking leads to new customers, and sometimes it just increases your knowledge. When you let someone know what you do, learn what the other person does, too. You never know when you may need to refer someone. Maybe you can help someone else gain some new business. Hopefully they too understand the scratching of the back principle. You want to build relationships with people. You throw some work their way, and they throw some work your way. A tried-and-true approach is that if you want business tomorrow, you need to build relationships today. There are many ways to network. Once you start and get good at it, you won't be able to stop yourself from doing it.

The more you to talk about your service, the more likely it is that someone will call you for your service. This doesn't mean that you should be self-centered and constantly talk about yourself, but recognize the opportunity to self-promote and network when it comes up. It can be as simple as telling people what you are doing and why you are doing it. Possibly toss in how you've trained for it, how you approach your endeavor, and how you are excited to help your customers. Networking also works in combination with other services. You may give piano lessons, and your best friend does house cleaning. Right after you give a piano lesson, the student's mom mentions that she needs to go home and clean up her house for a party and how she hates doing that. You pull out your friend's card and say, "I have a friend who can help you with that." Referrals by way of networking. Beautiful.

My goal in networking was always to get as many people as possible—after meeting me—to say to their friends, "Yeah, I know someone who cleans windows." Everyone likes to *know someone* who *does that*. The person you are talking to might not need your service, but his sister, mother, uncle, or grandmother might, which usually produces a referral. Be that go-to guy or gal. Everyone knows who the go-to people are. These are the people who get things done or have great knowledge on certain topics. Being the go-to person is a serious advantage when it comes to finding side jobs. If customers are used to going to you when they need help, you are now the first person they call. And being the first call is really important. When you are the first call, you have the advantage of closing the deal before anyone else has a chance. This isn't specific for networking either. *With any marketing, you are looking to be the first call.* [Sweet Tip]

Networking can start a powerful wave pool that results in referrals floating in. People like referrals. The person who refers your service gets a warm fuzzy because she helped a friend as well as you. And it gives the person who hires you a warm fuzzy because he's helping a college-bound student and using a friend's advice. Create that web or network of people who know what you do, and make sure they know you do it well. If that happens, you will start to see referrals. The great thing is that these people will seldom question your price; they will be happy they gave you some business.

> **Networking tip –** Realtors know everyone. Small business owners know everyone. Salesmen know everyone. Get the drift? Talk to your parents' friends, especially if they are in one of the professions mentioned above or something similar. These people make their livings off networking & referrals. They will understand what you are trying to do and since you have already impressed them by scheduling a meeting and telling them about your service in a professional manner, they will be more than happy to refer you. Leave them a stack of business cards and take a few of theirs as well.

Demographics

These are the characteristics of a human population. Demographics include gender, race, age, income, educational attainment, home ownership, employment status, and geographic location. These types of data are used widely in marketing.

What this means to you: Every service has a target demographic, which is those customers who are most likely to need or want your service. Babysitters target neighborhoods where there are lots of kids. Tutors and music instructors will look for school children. Landscapers and lawn mowers will target suburban neighborhoods with large yards. You will already know what your target demographic is from your training. You just need to cater your marketing toward that specific demographic.

While in high school and college, I would flyer neighborhoods with large homes that had plenty of tall windows. Someone who wants to teach piano will post flyers near the music room at school or talk to the music teacher. The Internet is yet again an excellent place to find your city or town's demographics. Another way is to drive around and find the best neighborhoods for your service. This can help steer you in the proper direction for advertising. A little preplanning for your advertising can go a long way.

Website

This is a collection of related web pages containing images, videos, or other digital assets. A website is hosted on at least one web server, accessible via a network such as the Internet.

What this means to you: Everything in the world seems to have a website. People, businesses, and organizations all utilize a website for marketing and informational purposes. A website helps customers learn more about you and what you do; it provides all of your information all in one place. Customers will often see an advertisement, say a flyer or sign, then go to your website to get more information. Your website is an excellent place to answer all the most common questions customers have. Your website should be well done and easily navigated. It doesn't need every bell and whistle, but there should be no typos and images should be clean and well laid-out. Who knows? If you do a good enough job building your own website, maybe that could be a side job for you as well.

Will a website bring in new customers? Maybe. But most likely your website will be more for informational purposes. I'm not saying you won't show up in a search; but the larger businesses in town that also perform your service are most likely throwing some of their advertising budget at search engine optimization, which means they will stay on top of searches. At this point we are trying to utilize the lowest-priced forms of advertising. First you buy the domain name, and then you buy a hosting package. There are any number of free site builders out there, and with a little searching you can find the right fit for you. Having a website isn't terribly expensive, but it's not free either.

Social media marketing

Social media marketing is the use of web-based and mobile technologies to turn communication into an interactive dialogue.

What this means to you: Facebook is an excellent way to advertise, market, network, and gain referrals. It's one of the most useful, if not *the* most useful, forms of social media marketing. What I like about Facebook is that trust and referral are built in. When your mother posts on her wall that her son is cleaning windows this summer (and of course she links the awesome Facebook window cleaning page you created for yourself), then her Facebook friend coworker hires you. Count it! New customer! We also can't forget other social media avenues like Twitter, LinkedIn, and YouTube.

Why not go totally free and use Facebook as your home base for information? From the standpoint of set-up and changing content, it's much easier to use than a website. Actually mirroring your information with your website is a good idea, however. You can use Facebook to network, advertise, and as a hub for referrals. Pictures, text…you can tell your whole story right there in one place.

Never forget about *your story*. As a student working your way through college, your potential customers might find it interesting that you want to be a finance major or a teacher or whatever you are going to receive a degree in. People will appreciate that you trained for a summer, that you love to play golf, etc. This isn't shameless self-promotion; its good business.

It's important for the customer to know who you are and what you do, both visually and verbally. That is called *personal marketing*. Keep in mind that you are marketing your service as well as yourself. Marketing yourself is a concept you will carry with you for the rest of your life. This is important because people buy from people. People buy from people they like and trust, even if it costs a little more.

Set up a Facebook business page. Why a separate Facebook page for your business? Why not use the personal Facebook page you already have set up? After all, you have over a thousand friends, right? The reason you set up a separate Facebook business page is because those thousand people you have listed as Facebook friends may not take working for yourself as seriously as you do. Do you trust that they will never post anything completely stupid on your wall? That's what I thought.

With a separate business page, you have more control over the content that is posted. Remember this page is for the benefit of your customers, not your friends. You will be looking for customers to *like* your page so that you can push content to them. Can you have your friends like your page? Absolutely. Just set those privacy controls so you can pull off any content your friends may post that doesn't fall in line with the image you wish to portray to your customers.

Here's an idea: Post a picture of you holding a squeegee with a caption that says, "School's out June 8. Who wants to be the first to get your windows cleaned on the 9th?" Then get your friends and parents to share it on their pages. Ask people to help you find more business. After your first job, post that you just cleaned a customer's windows and he or she is happy with your service. Ask that first customer to post a comment on your Facebook page as well as his or her own. You are now networking via social media marketing. Facebook has everyone in one location. Keep posting, keep sharing, and keep your Facebook activity up. In 2011 the fastest-growing demographic on Facebook was females between the ages of fifty and seventy. The largest demographic of current users is women between the ages of eighteen and forty. Coincidentally those demographics match most of the target demographics for most of the listed services in chapter 5.

Flyer

This is a single-page leaflet advertising a service or other activity. Flyers are typically used by individuals or businesses to promote their products or services.

What this means to you: Yes, flyers are old-school advertising when compared to Facebook; however they are a very cost-effective way of advertising that still works like a charm. A flyer gives you ample room to list who you are and what you do. It contains all the information you have on your business card—but on steroids. List your services. List how you want to pay for college. List that you have experience. List on your flyer that you are willing to do side jobs. Remember targeted marketing? Well, you choose the houses that get the flyers. That is as targeted as you can get.

We already talked about my window cleaning flyers. They were blue paper with one hand-drawn window and the caption "Residential Window Cleaning – Free estimates," along with my name and phone number. Simple as that. My marketing was completely built around that little blue piece of paper.

Should you go buy glossy, thick, professionally designed flyers? Not necessarily. When potential customers see a nicely done professional flyer like that, it raises their expectations. As a high school student, you are playing the Kid Card, marketing the fact that you are a motivated college-bound student trying to pay for school. Let the customer maintain a lower threshold of expectation. Go with regular paper and design the flyer yourself on your laptop, making it clean and typo-free.

Most people, especially those who have graduated from college, understand the effort and cost of going to college. Your self-made flyer will be well received. People want to help you. If they can get clean windows *and* help a student pay for school, it's the return of the warm fuzzy.

Here are a few basics you need to know about flyers and using them. These tips may seem pretty obvious, but sometimes it's the little things we overlook that cause the most problems down the road. A little common sense goes a long way here. Be honest about what you have to offer. Don't put something on your flyer to make yourself look better on paper than you actually are. Just be honest and up-front regarding your capabilities. If you are providing pet care in the form of dog walking and bathing, don't claim to be a dog groomer as well. You don't want to get into a situation where you have to clip a dog or cat's nails or cut a pet's hair when you have no experience doing so. Trying to figure such a thing out on the fly could turn into a bloody and painful mess for you and the animal!

Distribute your flyers where it makes sense to do so, and then repeat. Put your money where your mouth is; I mean, put your flyers where the money is, and do it often. Suburbs have easier windows to clean and, demographically, suburbanites have more money than residents within the city limits. Windows in suburbs are newer and are simply easier to clean. Flyering close to home is always a good idea, too. Neighbors may already know you or your older brother or your parents. This also cuts down on travel time and gas, both of which are expenses to consider. If you decide to paint, would you put the flyers in a brand new neighborhood? No. Find homes that are at least ten years old and in need of a good coat of paint.

In addition to passing flyers out door-to-door, post flyers in other targeted places, too. How about the coffeehouse where the school moms go after dropping the kids off at school or maybe at your parents' workplaces? I've never found posted flyers to be nearly as effective as those left door-to-door, but I'm a window cleaner. Every service is different, and marketing can be different for each service as well. I mentioned flyering over and over. Why would you flyer the same neighborhood over and over? If it didn't work the first time why would it work the third time? Here's why. Potential customers only hire you if there is an immediate need. If they see my flyer but don't need their windows cleaned, it will get thrown out. If they get the flyer and say, "Wow! My windows are filthy," they will call. People have needs at different times, so drop those flyers every couple weeks in the same neighborhood.

It may work something like this: Betty sees your flyer and pitches it in the recycling bin. Three weeks later she gets the same flyer, but this time she has a terrible smell coming from her garage and decides it just needs to be cleaned out. Here's a perfect side job for you. So she calls you because it says right on the flyer, "Motivated high school student looking to pay for college." Next thing you know, you spend two days cleaning out Betty's garage. She spends two days telling you what to pitch and what to keep. You build a nice customer relationship, the job gets done, and she pays you. A week later her best friend, Sally, calls you and says, "I need my shrubs trimmed because my husband broke his arm." Boom, another job. It started with a flyer, quickly turned into networking, and then resulted in a referral.

Here's a clever use of recycling. Why not put on your flyer: "Be friendly to the environment. If you have no use for this flyer, please place it in a paper recycling bin or, better yet, pass it on to someone who might be able to use my service. Thanks." By putting a message like this on your flyer, you're accomplishing multiple goals. You show that you're not only a motivated high school student but also environmentally conscious.

Flyer tip - There are rules when it comes to dropping and posting flyers. Putting a flyer in or on a mailbox is illegal. Believe me, from personal experience I know the local postmaster takes it much more seriously than you do. Some neighborhoods do not allow flyers. Some communities require a distribution license or permit. A quick call to the local municipality isn't a bad idea. The best way to drop flyers is to simply walk neighborhoods and put them on the front door. If you run into residents of the neighborhood don't keep walking by, stop and introduce yourself. You never know who is thirsty and wants lemonade that day.

Working the neighborhood to find opportunities

It's very important to market to your target demographic as well as hand business cards out to everyone you meet, but what about your own neighborhood? Should you also market in your own neighborhood even though it's not an ideal market for your demographic? Absolutely! Your neighborhood is always a good place to start. Your neighbors may know you and know what a hard worker you are. Or maybe you were the kid in the neighborhood who trampled everyone's flowers… it's lemons into lemonade time.

When you see that elderly neighbor who used to yell at you for trampling those flowers, walk up to him, put your hand out, shake your head, and say, "You know, I should apologize for my behavior when I was a kid. I hope my kid doesn't turn out that way. My name is…and I'm glad I'm not that kid anymore, and I bet you are, too." Then tell him what you're doing; and tell him if he needs you for anything, you'll do a little extra to make up for those years of trampling. By doing this you just showed someone that you are mature, and maturity scores big points with potential customers. Maybe you don't know your neighbors at all. Now is the time to expand your horizons and introduce yourself. Mention the fact that you should have introduced yourself years earlier. Say to them, "I was a shy kid, but I've outgrown that now." Even if your neighborhood isn't your target demographic, it's not going to hurt to have people you know in the neighborhood promoting your skills.

Start tag-teaming your advertising to cover more areas. If you're a window cleaner and your demographic is the same as your buddy the landscaper's, then maybe you two can double up on some marketing. I have done this before. When you go out on a sunny Saturday afternoon to drop flyers in a neighborhood, maybe you could drop one of your flyers as well as one of his. He can do the same, allowing the two of you to cover twice the area in the same amount of time. The customer who hires out landscaping most likely will also hire out window cleaning.

A sunny Saturday afternoon is the best time to hit neighborhoods with flyers. More people are at home, so Saturday afternoon sure beats Tuesday morning when everyone is at work and your chance of bumping into people is slim. Not that those Tuesday morning flyer drops won't generate opportunities. They will. I'm not recommending that you bother people during their family time, but when you do see a man in his driveway walk up and say with a smile, "I don't mean to bother you; but if you ever need me, please give me a call. Have a nice day." Then hand him a flyer. This approach is short and sweet and to the point. What that customer does next is look at your flyer. He will flash back to your presentation and, if he has any interest, call and talk to you about it. That might be all you need to do to pick up a new customer.

While handing out flyers, it makes sense to park on a corner to display the magnetic signs on your vehicle. People may be out for a walk, see the signs and say, "Ah, honey, put that number in your phone." Others may see you passing out the flyers and wonder about what you are doing. As a woman passes you on the sidewalk—because you are courteously walking the sidewalks and not walking through yards—she stops and asks what you are dropping on front porches. You hand her a flyer, introduce yourself, and the next thing you know you're talking like old friends.

This is old-fashioned selling and, man, does it work! When you see a nice and sunny Saturday afternoon in the forecast, get yourself ready, dress accordingly, wash the car, put a smile on your face, and go get some business. There is no better time to walk neighborhoods and find opportunities. I know, nobody wants to go door to door, but remember, "If you ever need me, please give me a call." How hard is that? This is just as easy as telling the clerk at the checkout to "Have a nice day." If you are shy, start practicing; and then get out there and market yourself.

Remember that all of these marketing strategies overlap. So let's say you've been referred to a customer via your mom's Facebook page. The customer lives in a neighborhood you are unfamiliar with. Why not flyer the rest of the neighborhood after the job is completed? Or better yet flyer the neighborhood when you do the estimate. Maybe you catch a neighbor outside and say, "Hi, I just looked at Mrs. Jones's windows and was wondering if you'd be interested in an estimate, too?" By doing this you save time and fuel costs. You've now just killed two birds with one stone.

Hopefully these folks know Mrs. Jones and can talk to her about how professional you were. Not only does this method increase productivity for the day, but it can be beneficial for long-term productivity as well. When the referrals and flyers work out and are in full swing, you can schedule multiple houses in the same neighborhood on the same day. With more houses closer together, you make more money in less time. Next thing you know, you are scheduling a whole week of work in the same neighborhood off a couple of flyer drops.

When the customer calls you

Answer the phone! {**Sweet Tip**} It's common knowledge that customers often purchase from the first service provider they talk to. When a customer calls looking for a service to be performed, he doesn't want to call everyone in the phone book; he just wants to talk to someone who makes him feel comfortable. After all, that customer simply wants a service done right and for a fair price. So what happens if Mrs. Jones calls for window cleaning, and she's comfortable with the first person she talks to on the phone? She will most likely hire that person, often regardless of the price, assuming the price is fair.

Is it important as a service provider to be the customer's first call? Absolutely! I've always said, "If I am the customer's first call, I will close the deal before the next guy even gets an opportunity." And, if you provide excellent customer service even before the sale, you are that much closer to collecting your money after the job is done. With any marketing or advertising, one of the main goals is to *be the first call*. Maybe the person is calling you first because someone referred you or because one of your marketing pieces attracted the person's attention. Regardless of the reason, there is a definite advantage to being that first call. I will go a step further. We live in an impatient society. If a customer calls and you don't answer the phone, the customer will call someone else and that guy gets the first chance to close the deal. Don't give that guy a chance; answer the phone.

Business etiquette

It's just a lemonade stand. Do we really need to talk about business etiquette? Yes, it is; and yes, we do. I've seen enough poor business etiquette from teenagers in my life to feel obligated to address it. If you already know all of this business etiquette stuff, then good for you. But it's not going to hurt to review. I see it this way: you can learn it now at age seventeen, or you can learn it after college at age twenty-three.

Customers will expect certain behaviors from you; and you will need, at the very least, to meet those expectations. We could get into the whole bit about the status quo and how the machine is set up to make you conform like a tidy little zombie, but we'll save that for *The Lemonade Stand Rebellion*. For now you can rebel all you want, but it's not going to help you pay for school.

Standards for behavior are much higher when you work for yourself. You are at the customer's door to conduct business, which means you need to act like someone who is standing at their door to conduct business. When you introduce yourself, stand up straight, make eye contact, smile, and put your hand out and say, "Nice to meet you." On the other hand, if you are a sandwich artist making $8 an hour working for someone else, your posture doesn't matter as much. At the sandwich artist job, you don't have to know how to shake hands. Eye contact is not required there either and very rarely does it occur, at least in my experience. But that is not you; you are the 10. So go through the next few paragraphs and make sure you can do the following:

Make eye contact

This is the one thing that I see people screw up all the time. People shake hands and look up, down, or around the room. The only place you should be looking is into your customer's eyes. It shows respect and lets the customer know you are serious. Whenever you are talking to the customer face-to-face, you should make eye contact. If you and the customer walk around the house to look at something in the backyard, then your eye contact isn't as important; but those face-to-face meetings require good eye contact.

The handshake

Shake hands firmly and use your whole hand. No soft, three-finger handshakes but no bone crushers either. You aren't trying to show Mrs. Smith that you can dominate her in an arm-wrestling match. You're simply showing her you have confidence and a sense of self. And I can't believe I'm saying this, but use your right hand. I met someone once who shook with his left hand. He thought he was being cool, but I found it incredibly awkward. The rule of thumb is right hand, one pump; up, down, release—the end. Don't stand there holding hands for a while gazing into Mrs. Smith's eyes. And, while we are on the topic of don'ts, here are a few more: Don't grab the person's elbow or arm with the other hand, don't do the half hug thing, and absolutely no fist bumping. Now if the customer does any of these, that is fine. But it's not fine for you to initiate it. I've met quite a few teenagers, and I'd say most have a poor handshake. My suggestion is to practice a few handshakes on your parents. Don't be embarrassed. If my son came to me and asked to practice handshakes, I would be ecstatic. And if your dad gives you the limp fish, teach him how to shake hands like a professional!

Verbal introduction

A short and simple greeting with your hand out works best: "Hello, I'm Geof White. Nice to meet you." Simple and polite. A big part of that first impression is your greeting. And don't forget to shake hands again when you leave. Accompany that parting handshake with, "Thank you for the opportunity. It was nice to meet you" or if you scheduled the job say, "Thank you, I will be here next Saturday at nine o'clock." If you go in there focused on being professional, you will speak like a professional and, believe me, the customer will notice.

Mannerisms and posture

Stand up straight. Yes, I sound like your mom, but I have no doubt that forty-five-year-old mother who tells her ten-year-old son not to slouch every day will notice your posture, too. Keep your hands out of your pockets. Standing with your hands in your pockets is too casual for a business conversation. Bring a pen and a clipboard with paper to make notes about the customer's needs. If you do this, your hands shouldn't even have the opportunity to find their way into your pockets. Even if you don't write anything down, you're prepared to and you look that much more professional. Try not to act nervous even if your palms are so sweaty that the previously mentioned pen keeps slipping out of your hand. Swaying or rocking back and forth is a definite no-no. It sounds weird, but it's very common for people to sway when nervous. Also, never lean on a doorway like you're perfectly at home. This shows a lack of respect for someone else's home.

> **Etiquette Tip -** Want to really impress the customer? Keep a pair of those surgical 'booties' in your pocket. You know, the blue or white shoe covers for your feet. If the customer invites you in, stop and put the booties on. I can't tell you how many positive comments I've received over the years for doing this. What you are doing is showing respect for someone's home and your customer will assuredly appreciate it.

Appearance matters

Let's say you go to your favorite restaurant and your waiter comes to your table with a certain unidentified funk all down the front of his shirt. This particular waiter hasn't shaved in a few days. By the looks of his hair, he hasn't showered either. His shirt, besides being covered in special sauce, is half untucked. He has a noticeable slouch, mumbles his words, and doesn't make eye contact when he speaks to you. After he takes your drink order, he runs his hand through his thick, greasy hair. As he rounds the corner to put in your order, you swear you see his finger go to his nose. Is this the type of appearance you want to see in someone who's about to bring you food and drink? I didn't think so.

Your outward appearance plays a major role in how you are perceived by customers. Put the tragus and septum piercings away for the time being, comb the Mohawk over or get rid of it completely, and look the part. Keeping your clothes and hair clean shouldn't really be an issue, but changing your hairstyle and removing piercings is a bit more personal. You'll land more customers without funky hair, a bunch of metal hanging from your face, and holes in your earlobes big enough to fit a football through. Think of this as an exercise in acting. You are now an actor and can be one person while promoting your business and a completely different person in your free time. Embrace this opportunity. Not everyone has the chance to be two different people, so have fun with this.

Your car

Wash it regularly, shine the tires and rims, and keep the dashboard and other inside areas looking clean. Don't keep old drink containers, fast food bags, old issues of *Forbes* and *The Wall Street Journal*, or any other kind of rubbish lingering week after week. Clean your car out at least once a week. If a customer or potential customer happens to approach you at your vehicle, what do you want this person to see: a clean and nicely maintained vehicle or a trash-laden, unwashed, and uncared-for vehicle? This is especially true if you have started any type of cleaning-related service.

Clothes

Keep them clean. Although holes in your jeans are sometimes fashionable, keep them to a minimum. Don't wear shirts with vulgar words or pictures or any other potentially offensive material on them. Although these are sometimes cool and can get your political/spiritual/social beliefs across in three words or less, keep them for nonbusiness time. This doesn't mean you have to dress uncomfortably or feel stuffy. Just try not to scare people. When you walk up to the door wearing a nice T-shirt with "John Smith, the window cleaner" on the front and back, a customer can't help but be impressed. An online printing company or even a local screen print shop can do single-color T-shirts very cheaply.

Simply dress the part. From your training you should know what acceptable dress is. When you are a music instructor, a tutor, or something similar, the way to dress is pretty obvious: conservative/casual. However, if you are a painter, it is perfectly acceptable to wear a painter's clothing. In fact it's better to wear the old painter's bib overalls. If you are a landscaper or gardener or something like that, the customer will expect to see you in a T-shirt and jeans or shorts. As I mentioned earlier, a T-shirt with a logo should suffice for most situations. Maybe with "Landscaping my way through college" on the back. If you do a service where you get dirty, keep a spare pair of shorts and a shirt in your vehicle. You just never know when you will need to throw on that clean shirt. Maybe you've been working all day and need to stop for an estimate on your way home. You may not smell like a peach anymore, or you're all dirty from climbing through bushes to get to some windows. But at least you can pull out that spare shirt and throw it on.

Advertising

Keep your advertising signs and anything with your name on it neat and clean as well. The whole intention is for a potential customer to look at your advertising and say, "I want to talk to that person about helping me." While a sign made with crayon and markers works great for an actual kid's lemonade stand, let's have all signs look as professional as possible for your endeavors now. And when a sign starts to look worn, replace it.

Tools

If you use tools in your business, the same principles apply. Keep them clean and in top working order. Keep your tools organized and readily accessible, too. There is nothing worse than searching your car for fifteen minutes trying to find that one special tool you need. Make sure your tools are always ready to perform their assigned tasks.

Driving up to the customer's house

The first impression is your arrival at a customer's house. You pull into the driveway, and before he ever sees you he sees your car. I understand that the car you drive was probably a hand-me-down and may not be the prettiest. Or maybe you're driving your family's wood-sided Griswold station wagon. There isn't much you can do about the car you drive—not yet at least—and customers know that; their expectations will be low. Maybe you have a magnetic sign on the side, unless there's too much rust or wood paneling, in which case you might be able to spray paint your sign on the car. That's a joke! Do not...I repeat, do not spray paint your car. Regardless of what you're driving, you can keep that vehicle clean. If you are a house cleaner, window cleaner, or anything else to do with cleaning, it's a must.

Here's a list of obvious don'ts when you pull up to a customer's house.
- Don't have your radio blaring music
- Don't spit your gum or anything else on the sidewalk
- Don't throw out trash
- Don't burp loudly
- Don't end any loud cell phone conversations with things you wouldn't say directly to the potential customer...things like, "Let me get this crap done, and then I'll call you and we can hook up."

Just because you don't see the customer doesn't mean she or her kids don't see or hear you. Be very mindful of using profanity even on a call before you go in. You want to avoid giving the customer any impression that this work is not important to you. Remember that you are there to conduct business. Present yourself like you are serious and ready to work.

Sales

Quite simply, sales is offering to exchange something of value for something else. The something of value being offered may be tangible or intangible. The something else, usually money, is most often seen by the seller as being of equal or greater value than that what he or she is offering for sale.

What this means to you: Did you even realize that you were selling when you handed those customers their lemonade? Every cup of lemonade is sold. Without selling, nothing gets sold; if nothing gets sold, no revenue is generated. If no revenue is generated, the lemonade stand folds and you can't pay for school. It's been my experience that most people hate the words *selling* and *sales*. What if instead of saying, "Go sell" I said, "Go tell people who you are and what you can do for them." Doesn't sound so bad now, does it? When you present information about who you are, what your skills are, and what you can do for a customer (selling) you are simply telling this person about yourself.

Back to selling, I can already hear some of you saying, "But I don't want to sell. I'm a computer person…house cleaner…painter, but definitely not a salesperson." Salespeople have a reputation for being less than honest or telling you *anything* to get you to buy. They're always looking to make a quick buck. Okay, if you don't want to be that way, simply *don't be that way*. Be honest about what you have to offer. The best salespeople are those who are truthful about what they sell. Again, don't think of it as sales. Get away from that word. Think of it as promoting your service, promoting yourself. If you just be yourself and explain to your customers what your services are, your pricing, and how you can help them, you are now selling without even knowing it.

Conveying your message to your customers may not be easy at first, and for some people it's never easy. For others, it comes naturally. Remember, *you* know *your* service and capabilities better than anyone. You merely need to convey to the customer how you can solve his or her problem. I've found that the best way for the beginner is to present it in a professional yet passionate way.

Sales as a second skill

Sales is one of the most important aspects of any business. The skill of sales is the most important second skill a person can have regardless of the profession. Keep this in mind for your profession after college. Whether you are a window cleaner, website designer, landscaper, or tutor, if your second-best skill is selling, you will always have work because selling brings in customers. Maybe it's not a bad idea to work on becoming proficient at selling while you work for yourself during your teen years, so that it's second nature once you have graduated from college and start your chosen professional career. Sales will be just as important then.

Reaction selling

After you have been working for yourself a few years, you won't have to focus on sales as much because you'll be reaction selling. This is the result of effective marketing. A customer calls—let's say she received your flyer and is reacting to the message on the flyer—and you just show up and present your information to her in a way that makes her want to hire you. Your marketing prompted the customer to call, so all you have to do is close the deal. This is much easier and less stressful than going out and initiating the contact by knocking on someone's door without being sure if the person needs or wants your service. With reaction selling you don't get quite as much exercise; but, hey, it's a fair trade. If you can master reaction selling and you are utilizing the right marketing, you will find yourself buried with work.

No one likes to be sold to, but everyone buys [**Sweet Tip**] so make them choose you. When a customer calls you, he is not calling to hire you—just yet. Initially he is curious about your service. Luckily for you, you're fishing for customers. Now you need to reel that customer in. So where do you start? Listen intently to your customer. He will tell you exactly what he is looking for. Every customer is different and they all have different concerns. Listening intently is a skill that will get you many places with many people in life. So turn down the chatter, stop planning what you're going to say next, and start listening.

If the person doesn't tell you what he is looking for in a clear way, just ask questions. Asking good questions will help you understand as well as impress the customer and keep the conversation going. The better the conversation, the more comfortable the customer will be with you and the more likely he is to hire you. Trust and comfort—remember that. Be truthful about yourself and your capabilities. Do this by identifying the customer's needs and providing the solution. Discuss what the customer can expect when you are finished with the job.

During this entire conversation, keep price out of it. When selling to a customer, try not to make it all about price. In fact, don't make it about price at all. Make it about the feeling the customer will have after you have alleviated his concerns. Say things like, "That will be a great view with clean glass!" or "You will have the cleanest windows in the neighborhood!" or "Your neighbors will envy your view of the lake when I'm done!" Too many times the person selling makes it about price: "I've got the lowest price around. I can beat anyone's price." Don't do that. By doing that you are devaluing your skill and training. You are teaching your customer to care more about price than quality. Sell quality, not price. Sell who you are and how you will do it, not price. Sell what the final result will be, which is selling value. If you sell correctly, the value will overshadow the price.

The price then becomes less important; it becomes just another detail to be sorted out like scheduling and how long the job will take.

You also want to let the customer know you are the best person for the job and that she will be happy with your work. Show self-confidence. When your interaction with the customer is over, either on the phone or in person, she should feel comfortable with you. Strive to be pleasant, knowledgeable, and serious about your skills. Do not be cocky or brag…these are common problems with young people and sales. They will turn the customer off.

The fear and avoidance of selling is where many people (your competition) will fall off. People simply don't want to do it or are too afraid to even try. Some are too shy or lack the confidence, especially at a young age. Again, it gets easier the more you do it. If you can get past the fear and master selling quality over price, you will have mastered a skill that will serve you well for the rest of your life. Selling is a transferable skill, or should I say that selling value is a transferable skill? You can take that skill with you wherever your career path leads. Your title may not be salesperson. But if you are an engineer and design a new robot, you had better have some sales skills when you demonstrate it to the investors. Teachers sell their curriculum choices to their administrators. A human resources director sells the company's new benefits package to the employees. Every job interview you go to in your life is you selling yourself to that potential employer—and the interviewer selling his or her company to you. Sales impacts everything.

Here are a few examples of what I would say to my customers. I found the easiest way to handle most customer questions was to use the same prepared sayings or lines over and over. Being consistent with your sales message is important for several reasons. Since you know that the message you are using works, why reinvent the wheel? Being consistent also helps when customers talk to each other and compare notes—because they will. You will find after a while that many customers have the exact same questions. That is why information on your website, Facebook page, and flyers as well as what you say in person or on the phone should be consistent. It will make your life easier in the long run, and it's also easier on you because you really only need to remember a few lines.

- "You won't even know I was here except that, when I leave, all your
- glass will be clean."
- "I like to clean your type of windows. They look so good clean. Look at that view!"
- If I see white carpeting, I always say, "I wear booties at all times inside your home."

- "Would you like me to clean out your gutters while I'm here cleaning the windows?"

If I see that they have a Frisbee on the roof I will say, "I'll make sure I get that Frisbee down for you. It'll only take a minute." And if you want to close the deal during the estimate, say this: "Mrs. Smith, I can jump up there and get that Frisbee down right now for you."

My first job after college

Like most people, after college graduation I started interviewing for jobs. One interview was in Grand Rapids, Michigan. I walked into the job interview fully prepared to answer the usual questions. I sat down and he asked me a few questions. At one point he looked at my resume' and asked, "If you have a Construction Management degree why don't you have any construction experience? Why didn't you work construction in the summers?" I said, "I clean windows in the summer." Rather unimpressed he halfheartedly said, "Tell me about that." I told him the truth: "I've cleaned windows every day of every summer since I was 16. I started cleaning windows for myself at age 17 and eventually I charged $50/hour and I was booked all summer." That perked him up a bit. "Tell me more," he said. So I proceeded with 'My Story' that you read at the beginning of this book. When I got to the part where I would come back from school each year and call all my customers to see if they wanted their windows cleaned, and asked if they knew anyone else who wanted their windows cleaned, he stopped me and said, "You're not a window cleaner. You my friend are a salesman." I will never forget that moment. He was right, and wrong. I was one a hell of a window cleaner but I had never thought about the fact that I was selling too. A big reason for my window cleaning success was because of my sales skills. It was my secondary skill. He offered me the job that day and I took it.

The sales pitch

"Good afternoon. Would you like a cup of lemonade? I'm selling lemonade for a quarter, and you can add a cookie for fifty cents." Yup, you need a sales pitch. Don't get all defensive. I'm not saying you should be like Crazy Eddie selling TVs at insane prices. I'm saying you should have a general verbal delivery explaining your service to prospective customers. First and foremost be yourself. And if you happen to be a little bit like Crazy Eddie, well, maybe tone it down a bit until you start making TV commercials. Remember when we talked about being honest about your capabilities and what you can do for the customer? That's the basis of your sales pitch. Tell customers what you can do and why you are qualified to do it: "I'm working this summer to pay for college, and I will do my best to make sure you are completely satisfied with my work." That's just honesty and a sales pitch that you practiced eighteen times in the car on the way to Mrs. Smith's house.

Great salespeople talk to themselves. Sounds crazy, doesn't it? It's not crazy. It's good practice. Salespeople will often go over what they're going to say before they walk in to talk to the customer. Being prepared is always your best approach. Remember those lines I used all the time? I used them a lot, meaning I practiced them a lot. Customers would always say to me, "Wow, you clean windows so fast!" and my line was, "You would, too, if you cleaned windows every day. I could do it in my sleep." My response isn't bragging. I'm saying that I'm a professional window cleaner, and professionals work at a quicker pace because it's second nature to us. After all, I practice cleaning windows all day, every day. I could have said, "I'm rushing to get to the next job," but obviously that's not a wise thing to say because it gives this customer the impression I'm not being thorough or I'm not concerned about her windows.

Stand-up comedians rehearse, actors rehearse, and sales people rehearse. I know someone who does a lot of presenting to small groups. She's a consultant and presents training classes to her clients. She told me once that the only way to develop confidence in a speaking situation is to gain more experience by practicing. This practice can be out loud to yourself in the mirror, to yourself in the car on the way to your meeting, or to your parents or little brother. Practice is the best way to build confidence as well as insuring that you sound like a professional.

All of this practicing and saying the right things leads to asking for the business. There is an old saying in the sales world: "You won't get the order signed unless you *ask* to get the order signed." People will say no and people will say yes. Sometimes the customer will just hire you; other times you will need to ask. Asking for business is perfectly acceptable. It's a hard thing to do at first but, like everything else, it gets easier. If you're having trouble or are a bit hesitant, here's a suggestion. Pretend you are asking your parents for the car keys. In your short driving career, I'm sure you have come up with a few creative ways to convince your parents to give you the car keys. There's no difference when asking for business. You want car keys? Ask. You want work? Ask. If you ask enough people for work, maybe you'll make enough to buy your own car and you'll never have to ask for the car keys again!

A few common sales *asks*:
- Do we have an agreement?
- Do you want me to start on Monday?
- Would you like me to put you on the schedule?
- Would you like me to take care of that for you?
- Would you like me to help you with your problem?
- Can I plan on assisting you with this?
- Can we agree to cleaning all the windows for $200?
- Can we consider this an agreement for services?

A common misconception for many people new to business is that once you ask and the customer says yes (also called closing the deal), the work is over. There is no need to keep marketing until you need more work. Not quite. The work begins when the marketing process begins. Should you keep marketing while you are busy working? Absolutely. Marketing is a constant process. To constantly have work, you must constantly market. It goes like this: Market, close the deal, perform the work, and go to the bank. Lather. Rinse. Repeat.

Ask for referrals again and again and again...

First I tell you to ask for business, and now I'm telling you to ask for referrals? Oh, brother, not again, right? The reason it's so important to ask for referrals is that it's extremely effective, regardless of how annoying or redundant it gets. Let me explain why asking for referrals works so well. Remember all those crazy dictators from history class? They knew about this flawed human quality most people have. Saying yes promotes a positive feeling inside. Saying no generates the opposite feeling. A positive feeling or a negative feeling, it's a pretty easy choice. I'm not saying that everyone will say yes, because they won't. However, if they see value in what you are offering, even a little, internally they want to say yes. It's human nature. It is your job by way of marketing, advertising, and selling to make sure that customer says yes when you ask.

Remember this: referrals are easier to ask for than business. When you ask for a referral, you are asking someone to tell his friends about you and your service. Referrals are free. If you ask a person to refer you to his friends, it doesn't cost him a dime. If there is no cost attached and people want to say yes, then why wouldn't someone refer you? He wants to refer you; it will make him feel good to help that ambitious high school student pay for school. So where's the glitch? Here's the glitch. Right next to that not-so-admirable quality of constantly seeking approval is that other not-so-admirable quality called forgetfulness. People get busy...and forget. People don't refer you as they said they would because they forgot. So how do we get around that? Easy. Be proactive.

Every year when I came home from college, my first order of business was to call all my customers. I'd call, remind them who I was, and ask if they wanted their windows cleaned again. When Mrs. Smith said yes, we would find a day that worked for both of us and I would schedule the job. I would then say, "Do you know anyone else who might like to have their windows cleaned? I would appreciate all the business I can get this summer." Rarely did anyone say, "No, I can't seem to think of anyone." It was almost always, "You know, my sister might like a quote." Here's where being proactive puts money in your pocket. Instead of saying, "Have her give me a call," I would say, "May I have her name and number so I can call her tomorrow?" Or "Would you be willing to call her today and let her know I will be calling?"

What I did was ask for a referral and then take the contact information. Taking down that contact info is crucial. If the customer forgets to call her sister and tell her about me, it doesn't matter. I will call her. What you don't want to do is let the customer be in control of your contact. Either the message never gets relayed, or she forgets to call her sister altogether. So when you ask for a referral, get that contact information right away. Keep the ball in your court.

Sometimes your customer won't immediately provide the referral information. In that case, follow up. For example, let's say you do a job for a customer and you ask for a referral. He says he knows a few referrals but doesn't have their numbers handy. Give that customer some business cards and, if you don't hear anything in a day or so, call back, e-mail, or Facebook him. Keep it fresh in his mind. Asking for referrals sounds like a little work, doesn't it? It is. It's also easier making those couple phone calls than dropping five hundred flyers and most likely more effective.

After some time the referrals will take on a life of their own, and you may not have to ask so much. From years of your asking for referrals, your customers will start referring you on their own and the number of referrals can grow exponentially. Say you ask one hundred customers for a referral during the course of the summer, which is basically asking for one referral a day. If each customer refers one friend, you now have one hundred new potential customers. If only half actually hire you, then you just picked up fifty new jobs. To pick up fifty new jobs from flyering or putting a sign out or handing out business cards will take significantly more effort than asking for a referral each day. Just imagine how much business you would have if you asked three people or five people for referrals each day of the summer? You could potentially pick up hundreds of new customers. Referrals are your most cost-effective form of marketing and will usually bring in the most new customers. Maximize your referrals, flash that Kid Card one more time, and watch the work pour in.

Customer expectations

Every customer has expectations when he or she hires you. It's up to you to make sure you know exactly what the customer's expectations are, so that you can exceed them. Exactly what does the customer expect? Not all customers are the same, so each customer will have different expectations. On the other hand, you will notice over time that most customers have basically the same level of expectation when it comes to a particular service. A great way to approach this is to think like the customer or, better yet, ask the customer what his expectations are before each job.

If you bid the job, you should discuss expectations at the time you bid it, then review when you actually start. The more jobs you do, the more you will understand what customers are looking for. Service providers are notorious for forgetting about what the customer really wants and just providing what they perceive the customer wants. After every job have a quick conversation with the customer and ask, "Were you satisfied with the work? Was there anything else you expected that I didn't do?" It will be helpful for the next job you do. Ask questions and listen to your customers. They will tell you what they expect. After that, it's just a matter of doing it. Learn from the first job and take the knowledge with you to the second job.

Meeting expectations isn't nearly as impressive as exceeding expectations. [Sweet Tip] Often this is done with very little extra effort. How do you exceed expectations?

Do what you promised, do it flawlessly, and do a little extra. If you're a window cleaner, make sure every window is perfectly clean. Make sure the screens are clean, put the blinds back where they were, and wipe down the sills and window cranks. You might even want to clean the bathroom mirror for free. If you dripped on the hardwood floor, clean it up right away. If you see your customer lugging the garbage out, stop what you are doing and run over to help. If you're a music instructor, let the your student's parents know you will give Johnny an extra ten minutes today to play a fun tune of his choice because you have the time. Basically you want to provide that little extra something that will keep your customers coming back.

Learn the dog's name

Want to impress your repeat customers every time? Learn the dog's name. Write it down the first time you clean their windows. (Yes, write it down because if you don't you will forget. Trust me.) So that when you go back to clean that house again you can glance at your notes on the way in and greet the customer and dog by name. Believe me, Mrs. Smith will be impressed!

Don't forget to look for side job opportunities

There is no better time to discuss side jobs with a customer than when you are working for her. Most side-job opportunities come from current customers who hired you originally for your core service. That service will provide most of your revenue and be the reason you establish a relationship with the customer in the first place—*getting your foot in the door* as I call it. Once customers find out that you are a hardworking, dependable, trustworthy student, they will find more jobs for you to do. Take advantage of that and make it a win–win. Often you won't even have to inquire if the customer might have more work for you; the customer will just ask you. Middle-aged and older people have figured out that some things are just best hired out. Their time is more valuable than the money it costs to hire someone. Some of the side jobs I picked up from window cleaning back in the day included painting houses, staining decks, landscaping, detailing cars, removing old carpeting, helping families move, and cleaning out garages and basements. I even refinished some kitchen cabinet doors, but that quickly went from a side job to a bad job.

What to do when you screw up

I totally screwed up the kitchen cabinet doors job. I didn't know what I was doing, was not prepared, and didn't have the right tools. It was a tough job, and I shouldn't have even attempted it. I was supposed to take off the cabinet doors, paint them, and put them back on. It sounded simple but didn't turn out that way. The whole thing just looked like a mess when I was finished. The paint job itself looked fine; but that extra coat of paint made the doors slightly larger, and they didn't fit right when I hung them back up. The customers were gracious and understanding about it. I played the Kid Card and admitted my shortcomings. They hired a professional to come in and fix what I had done wrong, and they remained my window cleaning customers for some time afterward. Let's learn from my screwup.

Whether it's a side job or not, if you find yourself in a similar situation where you make a mistake or damage something, there are a few simple steps to follow to ensure you don't endanger your customer's trust.

1. Admit fault and immediately let the customer know about the problem.
2. Apologize sincerely and explain what happened.
3. Offer to repair the problem and then do it regardless of the cost.
4. After the problem is fixed, apologize again and thank the customer for his or her understanding
5. Learn from your mistake and don't make it again.
6. Don't accept payment for that job.

Do not, under any circumstances, try to hide your mistake. [**Sweet Tip**] A customer will eventually find it. He or she may not know you did it, but *you* will know you did. The chances a customer will make you pay for damages, knowing you're a poor college-bound student, are pretty slim. On top of that, how much damage can you actually cause? I'm guessing in most instances it won't be much. You may, however, be in a position where you must forgo payment for your botched service. You may even lose a customer, but the value of a clear conscience can't be measured in money.

Customer feedback

A great way to capitalize on a job well done is to send a nice thank you card, e-mail, or Facebook message to your customer. Sell after the job is done? Really? Yes! Does it ever stop? The answer depends on how much business you want and how fast you want to achieve your financial goals. After a job is complete and your customer is more than satisfied because you exceeded her expectations, this is the best time to ask for referrals. I'm not talking about a hard sell here. I'm just saying incorporate the request for referrals into your thank you card. Something simple like: "Mrs. Jones, I want to thank you for your business. I appreciate the opportunity and am glad I could help you with your window cleaning. Please pass my cards out to your friends. Sincerely, Geof White." See, not so bad. The advantage to sending an actual thank you card is twofold. People don't send thank you cards often anymore, so there is a certain mystique to opening one. *Business cards also fit conveniently into thank you cards.* [**Sweet Tip**]

There is some trial and error to finding opportunities and customers. While one form of advertising works for one customer, it may not work as well for others. At this point I must refer back to the circular momentum graphic. Can you see how marketing, sales, advertising, and referrals all work together? How could customers not want to visit your lemonade stand with all of that going on? Mix together some forethought, positive attitude, and work ethic and you have one tasty glass of lemonade to offer your customers.

CHAPTER 6

How much can you get for a glass of your lemonade?

The moment you make a mistake in pricing, you're eating into your reputation or your profits.

–Katharine Paine, founder and president of The Delahaye Group

Setting your price

Your lemonade stand sign says 25 cents per glass. But how did you come up with that price? Why 25 cents? Why not 10 cents or 50 cents? While there are several factors that can affect a pricing strategy, for a lemonade stand that 25 cent price is simply derived from the current market price. If all the lemonade stands are charging 25 cents, then that is the market price for a glass of lemonade. Pricing your product or service is important. It's a major factor in your dollars per hour equation and you should consider it when you choose the service you will provide as well.

If you charge too little, you run the risk of not making enough. If you charge too much, you run the risk of not getting jobs. There are several influential factors in setting your price, and once you establish your pricing structure you can always change it if it's not working for you. The following are all factors you should be aware of not only when setting your price but when determining which service to offer.

Charge by the hour

The great thing about charging by the hour is that you always know how much your revenue is. Your revenue is the amount of money you actually collect from the customer. If you are a tutor, babysitter, or anything similar, you will most likely charge by the hour. You simply tell the customer what your hourly rate is, and when you start to work the revenue clock starts ticking. If you charge $25 per hour for your service and you work four hours, you charge $100 for that job. This is a very cut-and-dried approach. There is little room to increase or decrease your profits, although you can increase your earnings by simply working more hours. If there are extra items like supplies that you need to complete the job, they are simply billed in addition to your hourly rate. This is often called *charging time and materials*. You always know what your revenue is. And if your expenses are steady, you will always know what your profit is as well. The negative to charging by the hour is that your hourly rate is very much controlled by the current market rate. This means that if all the other math tutors charge $20 an hour, then you are most likely stuck charging around $20 an hour. Making $50 an hour is harder to achieve because customers sometimes have a hard time seeing the value in that unless your service is a specialty or niche service that normally commands that amount.

Charging by the job

Charging by the job means you will charge one price to complete that particular job. Regardless of how long it takes, your revenue will be the agreed-upon price. Your dollars per hour will vary with every job, which can be good or bad. This is how I achieved $50 an hour. I would bid a job for $200 and make sure I was finished in four hours or less. I became very adept at looking at a job, figuring out what was required, knowing my skills, and calculating how long it would take me to complete it. Charging by the job is also the easiest way to make less than you wanted to when things go wrong. There is more effort associated with charging by the job. With many service jobs, like window cleaning, landscaping, pet sitting, and snow shoveling, you will most likely need to discuss the job ahead of time and give the customer a bid or estimate. For now just be aware of the difference between charging by the job and charging by the hour. I used a mix of both. For some jobs I charged by the hour, while for most I charged by the job. Whether you charge by the hour or the job, there are some basic factors that affect what you charge.

Market price

Every service has a local market price, and it's very important that you know what that market price is. The market price is the fair price range that most people are charging for that same service in your area. Pay close attention when you are training to what the local market price is. You may think your lemonade is worth $1 a glass; but if there are three other stands in your neighborhood and they are all charging 25 cents, $1 is going to be a tough sell. Or is it? Are everyone's cups the same size? Does everyone have lemonade as sweet as yours? Does everyone include a cookie with each glass? Is everyone else willing to be a *carhop* and deliver the lemonade to cars as they pull up? You can charge that $1 per glass, but it's going to have to be the best damn lemonade in town. *People will only pay a premium if they feel it's worth it.* [Sweet Tip] Make sure your lemonade is worth it.

The market price between one math tutor and the next should be very similar, and the same goes for landscapers and car washers. Market price has much more of an effect on services that charge by the hour because the customer can easily compare your price to the next guy's. Judging market price on a service that charges by the job is more difficult for the customer. There may be established market prices on certain jobs if they are common, but every job isn't always the same. Rarely did I bid two houses that were exactly the same. So customers didn't really know what the market price was for cleaning their windows. I always knew it was to my advantage that the customer could not gauge my price against the market. *As long as the customer felt my price was fair, then it was up to me to get the work done quickly, efficiently, and perfectly, thus achieving a higher dollar-per-hour rate.* [Sweet Tip]

While a customer paying by the hour will balk at paying $50 an hour, the customer paying $200 to get his windows cleaned does not balk when the job is done in less than four hours because the $200 price is already justified in the customer's head. It's simply a matter of perception. Perception is reality to the customer, and reality to the customer means real expectations in terms of price. The key thing to remember when dealing with market price is to be fair.

Start-up costs

It's time to discuss the cost of starting up your lemonade stand. This time, though, your mother isn't buying the lemonade mix. With all this talk of making money, we can't forget that sometimes you will need to spend on things like tools, supplies, and other items in order to start working for yourself. Remember when you were training and you were using someone else's tools? Well, not any more. When I started cleaning windows on my own, I had to go out and buy squeegees, squeegee rubbers, scrubbers, sponges, soap, ladders, rugs, poles, and quite a few other items. Sometimes I went with the cheap tools, and other times I bought the best. Every service is different, and each requires a different arsenal of weapons to attack the job. From your training you should know what you will need and which tools to skimp on and which ones need to be of high quality.

It's a good idea to sit down and list what you will need and how much it will cost. You should do this every so often. I used to do it at the beginning of each summer. I would list all of the equipment I would need to purchase that summer so I could make an informed purchase. By making a list ahead of time, it won't be a surprise when you actually need to buy those items. It will also give you the opportunity to save up for some of the more expensive items and give you time to research which brand you want to purchase.

You will need to use some of the money you made training to buy these items, and knowing how much they cost ahead of time will take away that sticker shock once you start buying. Here are a few things that everyone will need. First, you need wheels. Unless you are in a place like New York City, you will need some sort of transportation. This can be the biggest hurdle for many of you. I actually bought my first car when I was fifteen, before I even had a driver's license. I had been working and saving for a year or two for that big first used-car purchase. If you don't own your own car and you don't have the funds to purchase one, then you are at the mercy of your parents. Whichever way you go, you will need to get around; so make that priority number one.

Your second priority should be business cards. You will need business cards to hand out to customers. Your third priority is a schedule book. "Oh, c'mon, Grandpa Leo, my smartphone does all of that." Sure it does. So does mine. I also go through one or two phones a year. Trust me, your phone will die the day before you have three jobs scheduled. So go old-school, write it down in your schedule book, and keep the book in your car—if only as a backup.

 Enter your start-up costs into the Gameplan.

Operating expenses

Operating expenses are slightly different than start-up costs and should be taken into consideration when setting up your pricing structure. Operating expenses are those items you need to keep working. As a window cleaner, I would go through about one squeegee rubber a day, so squeegee rubbers would be considered an operating expense. The gasoline, flyers, window cleaning soap, sheet music, rakes, paint brushes, computers, or whatever you use in your service are all operating expenses.

You will need to charge enough to cover expenses as well as make a handsome profit. Operating expenses are often called overhead. Services such as landscaping and window cleaning will have more overhead than math tutoring. Try to get a firm grasp of what your expenses will be. At first you will be guessing. By year four you will know exactly what your expenses are. Having more overhead will require you to charge more. If you mow lawns, you will be using fuel. Figure out how much fuel your lawnmower uses for each hour you mow. This will enable you to factor the cost of gas into every hour of mowing you plan on for your bid. In the beginning you simply want to keep expenses as low as possible. Buying a $300 ladder that you will only use for one job doesn't make sense, unless you are charging an extra $300 for that job. Buying a $150 ladder that you will use every day of the summer is a good expense. That ladder only costs you $2.50 a day. Keep expenses in the back of your mind—even better, keep them on paper—when you are bidding jobs.

The best way to handle both operating expenses and start-up expenses in terms of adding those costs into your pricing is to come up with an average cost per day of work. You can then break it down by the hour if you like or by the job. I used to break down the costs for five days a week all summer. Although I did sometimes utilize the equipment other than on summer days, I liked using the summer days as a baseline for my figures because it was easy. If you are a window cleaner in a southern state, where you can work year-round, you can adjust the days you work to include those nonsummer days as well. Here's an example for a window cleaner who works sixty days in the summer:

Start–up costs		Operating expenses (total costs for the summer)	
Ladders	$250		
Squeegees	$100		
Misc. tools	$100	Fuel	$600
Business cards	$100	Soap	$ 30
Flyers	$200	Tools	$200
Rags	$ 50	Squeegee rubber	$ 70
Total start up:	$800	Total operating expense:	$900

Breakdown by day

If you work 5 days a week all summer, then you are working roughly 60 days.
Start-up: $800/60 days = $13.30 per day
Operating expenses: $900/60 days = $15 per day
Conclusion: Your costs are $28.30 per day for that summer.

Breakdown by hour

If you work 5 days a week all summer (60 days) at 8 hours a day, then you are working 480 hours.
Start-up: $800/480 hours = $1.69 per hour
Operating expenses: $900/480 = $1.88 per hour
Conclusion: Your costs are $3.57 per hour.

You can now add those costs into your pricing. If you price by the hour, you can simply add $3.57 to your per-hour goal. I would round that up to $5 per hour because there will be unexpected expenses, and a round number is much easier to deal with. If you have a niche service and you want to make $50 per hour, then you need to charge $55 an hour. If the market price is $50 an hour and you need to stick with that, then you must be able to accept $45 per hour for yourself. If you bid by the job, then estimate how long it will take you to do that job and simply add the daily amount. If the job will take you one day, you add $28.30 to the price of the job. If the job will take you half a day, then add $14.15 to the job price. Again, you should round that up to make it easy on yourself.

If you are going to do a service that requires costly equipment, such as lawn-mowers, power equipment, or other big-ticket items, then you want to take those averages over a few years instead of one summer. Larger items like this are built to last for years and often require some maintenance. Don't forget that those mainte-nance costs are also considered an operating expense.

 Enter your operating expenses into the Gameplan.

The law of supply and demand

What you thought was a boring concept in econ class is very real when you work for yourself. Supply and demand will affect your pricing and how many jobs are available. If there are fifty window cleaners in your small town, the market price for window cleaning will be lower than if there are only two window cleaners. I was able to charge my $50 per hour for several reasons. First, the Kid Card. Second, window cleaning is a niche skill; there weren't many people who could do it, especially if high glass was involved. Third, there were a lot of dirty glass opportunities (demand) and not enough window cleaners to keep them all clean (supply).

On the other hand, if you mow lawns and the other five teenagers in your neighborhood also mow lawns, you will see the prices and opportunities for mowing going down. This is simply too much supply for the demand. All it takes is for one lawn mower to drop his price to get a job, then someone else follows suit, and all of a sudden the market price is driven down. Less supply and more demand means you have the opportunity to charge a little more than if the situation were reversed. It's very important to find a service that has high demand and low supply.

High side of the *fair range*

A customer will only hire you if she sees value in what she is going to hire you for. Translation: she perceives your price as fair for the work you will perform. The thing to focus on here is that customers don't necessarily know what the market price is, but they will have an idea of what is a fair range to pay for the service. Your customer may have a preconceived notion she got from a friend who had a similar service done, or she may simply be guessing that it might cost a certain amount. A customer may think that $100 to $150 is fair to clean her windows.

A good bidder will price that job at $140 or $150. If you are proficient at your skill, then bid on the high side of the fair range. That customer is comfortable with $100 as well as $150, so go for the higher price. How do you know what the customer thinks is fair? Well, if she doesn't tell you (and sometimes a customer will), then you need to know your market price. If you stay on the high side of the market price, then you will be just fine. After all, you have trained, you paid attention learning, you are proficient, and you are going to do a little extra to make sure the customer is completely satisfied with your work. And you are holding your Kid Card up high for all to see. So charge accordingly and preferably on the high side of the fair range.

Pricing in the beginning

Here's where I go back on everything I just said, but only briefly. When you price your first couple of jobs, you may have a hard time commanding the high side of market price. You haven't worked for yourself yet, you may not be very efficient, and your customers at this point are guinea pigs. (Yeah, don't say that to them.) In the beginning your main focus should be getting as many new customers as possible so you can start that referral network moving. Time to make some deals. You will have to work for a little less in the beginning until your name gets out there as someone who does a fantastic job.

As your reputation and confidence grow, so will your prices and the size of your customer list. If you charge by the job, your prices will increase simply due to increased efficiency. Those $20 per hour jobs I did my first year were $40 per hour jobs a couple years later because I was so much more efficient and got the jobs done faster. Don't stress the lower prices in the beginning; just be aware. As time goes by and things get easier, start raising your price. And whatever you do, don't maintain the lower pricing for very long. It's easy to give your customer low prices now, but it will be hard to write that tuition check when you don't have enough in your checking account because you didn't charge enough.

Pricing side jobs

While you may have a firm grasp on pricing for your main service, pricing a side job can be challenging. You may not know how long it's going to take or even know all the variables involved. You may not even have a clear understanding of what the customer is looking to have done. All of which makes charging by the job tough. If you see that it's a small side job like trimming a couple bushes, cleaning out some gutters, or staining a small deck, you may be able to put a price tag on how long it will take. But if a customer throws out, "Would you clean out the garage for us?" and you can't even walk through it, you need to charge by the hour.

Charging by the hour is safe and probably a good idea for most side jobs. Again, these side jobs most likely won't bring in the dollars per hour like your main service; but remember the goal with side jobs is to make more than the guy slapping sandwiches together. So what do you charge for these side jobs per hour? My first thought is *as much as you can get,* but that is not specific enough. In the real world, people are used to paying $75 per hour for a mechanic, $25 an hour for a house cleaner, and $15 per hour for lots of other services. I would say that most side jobs will fall into that $15 to $25 per hour range. The difference between $15 and $25 may be how hard that particular side job is. If it's raking leaves, you may be stuck making $15 an hour. If you are helping someone move and there is a lot of furniture, you may want to charge $25 an hour. If you tell the customer $25 and he balks at it, you can either lower the price or justify why you picked that price by saying, "Moving a refrigerator is hard" or "Your gutters are forty feet in the air." Maybe the customer is comfortable paying you $20 an hour. I know it's not your ideal price, but it's not that bad either. It's more than twice what your buddy the sandwich slapper is making.

Do-anytime jobs

One summer a couple hired me to paint all the windows on their house. There must have been forty or fifty that needed painting. Some needed more attention than others—glazing, sanding, etc. I explained the variables involved to the customers, and we agreed on a price for the whole job. The woman said it didn't matter when I completed the job or how long I took, as long as I finished before the end of summer. So, when I wasn't cleaning glass, I would go over there and paint some windows.

What I remember about the job was that no one was ever home, which you will come to appreciate after you've been in enough homes with televisions blasting away, children screaming, and funny smells coming out of the kitchen. Not to mention the dog that barks incessantly at you. This wonderful empty house was in the woods near Lake Ontario. I would crank up the radio and paint away. It was a dream job with no boss, just painting away listening to tunes, working on my tan, and paying for college! If I remember correctly, that job paid around $1,500 just for the painting. And of course I cleaned the windows after I painted them. That was big money for a college kid then, and it's still big for a college kid now.

What I learned from this *do-anytime* job is that you can jump to it when you aren't busy. Because, let's face it, no matter how well you schedule things there will be holes in your work schedule. Customers reschedule, the weather may not cooperate, or maybe nobody wants their windows cleaned on a Friday afternoon before the holiday weekend. In fact, I did most of the painting over a Fourth of July weekend. I had no holiday plans, and I had no other jobs booked that weekend because of the holiday. So I painted. I was managing my time wisely.

There is also a double-edged sword factor to keep in mind when it comes to do-anytime jobs. Teenagers tend to procrastinate, so the do-anytime job becomes the I'll-do-it-later job until it becomes the hits-you-like-a-freight-train-at-the-end-of-the-summer job. The result is the job gets rushed at the last minute and you sacrifice quality. So if you do pick up a do-anytime job, be consistent with it. Manage your time. Even if you can only put in an hour here or there, do that as much as possible. The more you chip away at one of these jobs the faster you get paid. Besides, once you complete that do-anytime job, you should be looking for another one so you can keep those slow days filled with work.

Bidding by the job

This can be one of the more challenging concepts to learn when it comes to working for yourself. Back when you were training, you saw how jobs were completed, how jobs were approached, and maybe even how much the final invoice was. But how did the estimator or bidder come up with that price? Was it a guess? Is there a secret formula?

Having bid thousands of jobs, I can tell you that when you first start bidding there is a significant amount of guessing going on. However, as time goes by, you bid more and the guessing becomes educated guessing. Then, after even more time, there's no more guessing at all. After a couple years, I was able to arrive at a house, do a walk around, and know exactly how long it would take and what the price should be. Let's break it down so you can move from guessing to educated guessing as quickly as possible because, quite frankly, guessing will be a slower road to $50 per hour.

There are several ways to bid every job, and I will often bid jobs a couple different ways just to see if the bids are as consistent as they should be. I may bid one job three different ways and all the prices are about the same. In that case I know I bid it right. I may bid it three ways and the third way is completely off in price compared to the other two. So a double-check is in order. Or maybe all three ways yield drastically different prices. If this happens you really need to look at the job again and see what you are missing. Bidding one project three different ways is simply a system that will help you catch your own bidding mistakes.

> **Bidding tip** – Write it all down and take some pictures! Taking good notes when bidding will be an enormous help regardless of what method of bidding you are using. When you look at the building and decide to break it into sections– write it down and take pictures. I have made this mistake before. I look at a building and figure out a way to section out the building and then I sit down later to put some numbers to the sections and I can't remember how I sectioned it off. Write down anything and everything that may affect your workday – anything that you see as a potential problem, your window count, the tall bushes, the barking dog, anything. When bidding, the more information the better.

Factor bidding

How long does it take for you to clean a window? Time yourself. Get a watch (yeah, they still exist). Don't use your phone. It's a waste of time to take your phone out, ignore the new Facebook posts, and click on the stopwatch app. Put a watch on; and every time you do a basic window cleaning task, time yourself. I used to time myself cleaning windows all the time (no pun intended). For a window cleaner, the following process happens all day long: walk up to a window, scrub, squeegee, detail with a rag, clean the sill, and do a quick once-over with the eyes to make sure it's perfect. Done. The variable is what type of window, use of a ladder or not, climbing over bushes, etc. So you want to time yourself in different situations. I would time myself doing commercial glass standing on the ground, then on a ladder. Residential with storm windows and residential with screens. French doors. Don't fool around when you are timing yourself. Be as efficient as possible. No texting, no admiring the view off the ladder. Just complete the task and check your time. Then write it down.

Carry a small notebook and write down your times as well as any variables. Time yourself doing storm windows several times so you can get a good average. The reason you are doing all this timing is to establish exactly how long it takes you to complete a basic task that will be performed over and over. Once you know exactly how long that task will take, you can apply a price to it. You will then carry a master list of common tasks, how much time they take, and how much to charge for each. This concept will also apply to tasks that are similar to the timed task but not exactly the same. Every job is different. But if you know it takes you four minutes on a residential job to move a ladder, clean the window, and move the ladder again, then you can assume that the same time will apply to a commercial window using a ladder.

Here's an example. For some houses you have to disassemble the storm windows, clean the windows, clean the storm windows, and then put them all back together. If you can do one window in less than fifteen minutes and your revenue goal is $50 an hour, then you can clean at least four of these an hour. So $50 divided by four is $12.50 per window. So do you charge $12.50 per window? No. You charge more than that. You need to be compensated for your time and overhead costs that are not directly related to cleaning that piece of glass. Things like bidding time, ladders, gas for the car, flyering, etc. So you add an extra $2.50 per hour, thus resulting in charging $15 per set of storm windows. If the house has twenty sets of storms, then you charge $300 for the house.

This is called *factor bidding*, which is simply taking an established price (say $15 for a set of storm windows), counting how many sets of storms there are, and multiplying it out for the total price. If you are charging, say, $5 for a standard casement window, then you multiply the number of casement windows by $5. I used to keep a master list of prices on a form for the various types of windows. When asked for a bid, I would whip out my list, count the windows, calculate the factors, and there was the price. This is a very common form of bidding utilized by many trades out there. It works especially well if your skill is somewhat repetitive, where you are performing the same basic tasks over and over.

Section bidding

I have run into bidding situations where projects are either very large or have too many variables to use factor bidding. This can be quite intimidating because underbidding a large project is going to hurt more than underbidding a small project. The approach to take on jobs like this is to break the project down into smaller pieces. By doing that you are now bidding on a group of smaller areas that are easier to put a number to. You may actually utilize different bid techniques for each section. This can be done in several ways and every job is unique, so let's look at some examples.

A landscape customer calls and wants pricing on mowing, fertilizing, fall leaf cleanup, hedge trimming, and brush removal. This is a perfect time for section bidding. You want to figure a price for each specific task individually. You may want to list them out individually on the proposal, too. You may bid the fertilizing as a per-trip charge, meaning you will charge a certain amount each time you fertilize. Conversely you may charge fall cleanup on an hourly basis because there are too many variables. If you have to bid inside and outside window cleaning on a very large building, you may need to break the job down a different way to section bid it. Maybe the building has an enormous entryway full of glass. Bid that entry separately. Then take the four sides of the building and break them out separately. Now you have six to eight smaller sections to bid, which is much more manageable.

Gut-feel bidding

Sometimes when you are bidding a job, you will look at it and say to yourself, "That's only going take me an hour." As unscientific as that is, you can bid many jobs this way. Especially if they are small. Many times you will see a small job that is very similar to something you have already done, and instead of going through and counting every last piece of glass you can just use that old job as a reference for price and time. If it took you an hour to do that at Mrs. Jones's house and Mr. Johnson's house is very similar, then you know it will take you an hour.

Now the danger in bidding this way is that sometimes you have a tendency not to look at the job close enough, thus missing some details that may end up causing you to underbid. Many times I will write down what my gut tells me first, then go through the process of factor bidding the job to see if my gut was right. If the two bids are off by quite a bit, then I need to look at the job again and see what

I missed. Gut-feel bidding is an educational process that takes time, and there is a significant amount of trial and error. Try to stay away from this type of bidding until you have some good experience and feel comfortable bidding this way. Of all the ways to bid, this one is the most likely to get you into trouble.

The optimist in you

When you are an optimist (and many entrepreneurs are), you have a tendency to always look at the best-case scenario for every job. But that's not reality. Reality is that problems arise. Things take longer than expected. It happens to everyone. You need to learn from it, expect it, and not let it happen again. When you look at a job, include some time for problems. Then make sure the job gets done without any problems.

It's okay to say "No, thanks"

At this point I feel obligated to say that if you are asked to bid a project that you are not comfortable bidding because it's too big or too complicated, then don't bid it. It's perfectly okay to tell the customer that it's beyond your capability. And doing so will most likely save you a massive headache. It's those complicated jobs that often end up underbid, and jobs that are underbid are like being bitten twice. The first bite is that, whatever time it takes to complete, you will end up working for far less than your dollars per hour goal. The second bite is that while you are working cheap, you could have been working for your desired dollars per hour.

The backup: bidding by the hour

Watch for jobs with too many variables. They come up, so be prepared. A potential customer will ask you to bid something that is a little different than what you are used to or it's a really big project. Or you can see that things could change as the job progresses. Or the customer simply doesn't know exactly what he wants you to do until you get into the job more. It's your responsibility to recognize that you can do the job but that it's too hard to bid for whatever reason.

This is where you deviate from giving the customer a firm price and default back to an hourly rate. While the basis of this whole $50 per hour idea is to bid the job, work as efficiently as possible and come out at $50 an hour, sometimes that just isn't the way it's going to work. Instead of guessing on the bid and then making $10 an hour because you underbid it, go with a safer way. Be straight with the customer and tell him that due to the many variables and possible changes in the job as it progresses, you have to give him an hourly price. That way you are protecting yourself from the job from hell. You may have to quote it at $40 or even $35 per hour to get the job, but it sure beats that $10 an hour it might have been.

Change in *scope of work* and what to do about it

Here is another *It will happen, so be prepared* situation. You bid the job, show up to do the job, and the customer starts changing things—either adding work or asking for a little additional help here and there. It starts like this: "Geof, while you are up there cleaning that window, can you please dust off the ledge? (Which I would do at no charge anyway because it takes about one minute—remember to always do a little extra.) Next it's, "Geof, while you are here with that ladder, can you just paint that spot above the garage? It'll only take you a minute." (Which of course it doesn't.) It takes a half hour because you have to paint it, wash out the brush, put the paint away, etc.) Then she says, "Geof, can you help me for a minute get some boxes down from the shelves in the basement?" And now you are doing every little job she can think of. There is no problem with that, as long as you are charging for it.

The best way to approach it is to just say something when the customer starts asking for extras. Simply say, "I'd be happy to do a little extra for you, but I will have to charge if it takes more than five or ten minutes." Or if you know the task won't take too long, just say, "Throw an extra $20 on top of the bill for me and I'll take care of that for you." Those are fair things to say to the customer. And I'm not saying all customers will take advantage of you because most are not trying to.

You have to think like the customer for a minute. That seventy-year-old customer has a strong young man at the house doing work, and there are probably quite a few things that need to be done; but physically the customer has not been able to do them. So it's natural that while you are out cleaning the windows, the customer is thinking of these things. In the customer's mind, it's only more work; and you are already there. You simply need to make clear up front that you will be charging for extras. What you don't want to do when someone asks for extras is say that it's no problem; do the eighteen minor tasks that take you an hour; and then, at the end of the day when you go to collect, say, "I have to charge you an extra $50 for all that extra work." Because some people may have interpreted *no problem* as meaning that you'll throw that in for free. *Be up front about pricing, and it will alleviate a lot of headaches later.* {Sweet Tip}

Bidding recurring jobs

A few notes for when you are bidding jobs that you may do on a recurring schedule. Say you are going to mow someone's lawn once a week or clean the windows once a month. You will still go through the process of bidding, but you will need to take into consideration a few more factors. A repetitive job will get easier the more times you do it. You will naturally become more efficient at doing that task, thus taking less time. So the price of that first window cleaning may give you a lower per-hour rate than the subsequent window cleanings. Also, any time you clean something that first time, it may be very dirty because it hasn't been cleaned in a while. But if you are cleaning it once a week, then it won't be very dirty because you just cleaned it a week before. Again, taking less time and causing a positive shift in your per-hour rate. The customer for this recurring job may want you to come at a certain time each week. You need to be very cognizant of that fact when scheduling other jobs. Those recurring jobs are wonderful in terms of cash flow and marketing. There is guaranteed income, and you do not need to go out and market to get that next job. It's already scheduled, and you are familiar with the job because you've done it. The one thing to watch (again) with recurring jobs is underbidding.

Underbidding a recurring job means you are now doing that job for less *every time*, which is completely demoralizing. All of a sudden, you have a monthly job scheduled; and after doing it a time or two, you realize that you underbid it. And no matter how hard you try, it will always take you longer than you expected when you bid it. So what do you do now? You have a couple options. One is to tell the customer you screwed up and you will need to charge more. Don't expect a positive reaction from the customer. Once a customer has that value established in his head, your raising the price will wreck that. The other option is to suck it up and do it. Now if it's only a slightly lower per-hour rate or, say, it still works out to more than $15 per hour, then realize that it's still more than your friends are making. So you may want to just live with it. If the price was totally off the mark, the third option is to tell the customer that you can't do it anymore. He will ask why and you should tell him. Again, he won't be happy, but you are in this for the money to pay for school. You are not in this to work for nothing.

What you don't want to do in an underbid situation like this is to skip things or cut corners. It doesn't work. The customer will notice, and your reputation will be tarnished. Cutting corners goes against everything we discuss in this program.

The cost of bidding and marketing

You might ask, "If it takes an hour to bid a job, doesn't that affect my dollars-per-hour once I get the job? After all, I had to take the time to talk to the customer, walk around the job, take notes, ask questions, figure out a price, and present it." Correct. And if you go one step further, there is the time and money spent marketing to find that customer, too. These costs should be figured into every bid. Often bidding time and marketing expenses is simply seen as an operating expense and is entered into the equation as such. But there are several ways to do it:

- Example 1: Add 5 cents to every glass of lemonade.
- Example 2: Add $20 to every job you bid.
- Example 3: Add $1 to every window you bid when factor bidding.
- Example 4: Increase your hourly rate from $45 to $50 because you know that it costs you $5 an hour for bidding time and marketing expenses.

You will figure out which is the easiest for your situation. I will warn you, however, don't let the customer know you are adding to the price for bidding time. Most customers think a bid should be free. After all, you advertise *free estimates*, right? That's why you never list out your bidding costs to the customer. The customer only needs to see the total price for the job. What you do with expenses behind the scenes is your business, not his. *The customer needs only to see the price for the job and what you will do for him.* [**Sweet Tip**] Letting the customer know how you came up with that price will not be to your benefit.

Your value and pricing

Keep in mind your personal value when you set prices and bid jobs. Your time and knowledge are valuable. It's easy to give the customer a low price, but it's not easy to pay for college if you always give low prices. Get a good, fair price in your head to charge for every hour you work. Make sure that fair price covers your start-up costs and operating expenses and generates a significant profit. Enough profit to achieve your financial goals. It's up to you to find customers who will pay it and then prove to each customer your value. It starts with your first contact with the customer. Maybe a flyer or a referral or she saw you working down the street. Then the first phone call or personal meeting. Next the estimate, the job itself, and the follow-up thank you letter. Every point of contact (often called *touches*) contributes to what the customer perceives as your value. The more value the customer sees in you, the more you can charge and the easier it will be to pay for college.

Value is the difference between the anticipated price and the actual price. If the actual price is lower than the anticipated price, the value is perceived as good.

There is no profit in lowering the actual price; you must raise the anticipated price.

–Roy H. Williams, *Wizard of Ads*

CHAPTER 7

Squeeze faster, squeeze smarter…more cups = more cash!

Profit is *not* a four-letter word

The concept of profit can be a tough one to grasp at first. Not from the definition standpoint. Profit is what's left after you subtract your expenses from your revenue. It's simply the amount of money you get to keep. In this case the profit is the amount that will pay for your college education. What I'm talking about is: How much profit is acceptable? Does making too much profit make you greedy? Is there such a thing as too much profit? How much profit to expect depends heavily on how much you charge, how much you work (revenue), and how little you spend (expenses). From the Gameplan worksheet, you should have a good idea of what your profit will be. So why did I mention the concept of how much profit is acceptable? Because some people get weird when it comes to profits, especially people who don't work for themselves.

You built the lemonade stand, you made the lemonade, and you stood out there serving all day; so you should determine how much profit you make. Your time is valuable, and you should value your time. Your profit is just that: your profit. It is nobody else's business what your profit is. Only you are the judge of whether your profit is too high or too low; and, believe me, you will know if it's too low. That fact will surface every time you work and every time you pull out the calculator to figure out how much you made that day. If your profit is too low, you will start saying to yourself, "I work that long and that hard and make this little" or "It's not worth it."

There is also the opposite end of the spectrum. For some reason people seem to think that if you make too much profit you are being greedy or cheating or gouging your customers. To that I say, "Absolutely not!" If you are charging a fair price, bust your hump to get it done, do a great job, and the customer is happy, then a high profit is what you deserve! Remember when we discussed the fact that, if you are going to work for an hour, then make it worth your while? This is where you benefit from that theory. Make as much profit as you can every hour you work. It's not greed. It's good business. Profit is not a four-letter word.

Granted, factors like market price and the law of supply and demand will cap your potential profit, but everyone has a different perception of how much money you should make. The only person who should really know or care is you. I had someone say to me once, "You make too much money cleaning windows." To which I replied, "Do you think my prices are unfair?" She said, "No, the price is fair for cleaning my windows. But you were done in two hours, so you are making $50 an hour; and that's too much." Her perception was drastically different from mine. I found revenue of $50 per hour to be perfectly acceptable, most of which is profit because I had low expenses. In actuality I craved that $50 per hour revenue. Once I had it set in my mind that I was worth that much, why would I work for less? According to that lady, I should be working for less. Although I would never say it to her, she was wrong. In my mind I was worth every penny of that $100 it took me two hours to make. Working for yourself is about you and your desire to graduate debt-free. Profit is how you achieve that financial goal, so don't let other people's ideas or perceptions slow you down.

You should expect your profits to be far less in the beginning, compared to years down the road. In the beginning you have start-up expenses; and if you need power equipment or other expensive supplies, it will cost you even more. In the beginning work may seem scarce, and you may even take a few jobs that don't pay very well just to get your name out there. After four years it will be a completely different story. Your equipment will be paid for, you are charging on the high side of the fair range, you are booked up every day, and you're running every job at peak efficiency. So don't sweat the profit in the beginning. It might not be very pretty at first, but with conscious effort it will go up significantly. Remember the inverse proportion graph?

Because your profit is the very bottom number of this math equation that we call working for yourself, it is affected by every single aspect of what you do every day when you work. If you take a break, stop to check your messages, get lost driving, or underbid a job, your profit will suffer. On the other hand, there are things you can do in a day that will increase your profit. Let's consider working at maximum efficiency, multitasking, and scheduling two jobs right next door to each other to limit travel time. You got it. They all result in higher profits.

I am going to advise against nit-picking every little thing those first two years. In the beginning you should be concentrating on doing your best job every time and exceeding customer expectations. You really need to make sure you are serving the best damn lemonade in town so you can give yourself that raise from $20 per hour to $50 per hour. Over time, as that gets to be second nature, you can start working on different aspects to increase your profit. Again, this is much easier to do if you are charging by the job. When you charge by the hour, there are fewer variables you can change and therefore fewer chances to increase profit. If you are charging by the job, anything you can do to be more efficient will increase that profit.

Maximizing profit

After you have the bidding down pat, maximizing your profit can occur in a number of ways. With each successive year you work for yourself, the ease with which you maximize profit will increase. One easy-to-understand method to make more money in less time is to simply *speed up*! After doing the same motions over and over, your body and mind can perform certain tasks almost literally blindfolded. Through repetition our muscles (your brain is a muscle, too) retain the motions of the same action so that performing the action becomes almost effortless. Ever driven a car and time gets away from you? All of a sudden, you've arrived at your destination and you don't even remember how you got there? That's kind of the idea here. After a certain point (some say after ten thousand hours a person becomes an expert at any task), you can be on autopilot while doing your job. That's all fine and dandy, but you don't want to just do the job at autopilot speed. You want to harness the autopilot and consciously make the decision to move a little faster. This does not mean cutting corners in order to give the appearance of moving faster either. Let's bring out yet another window cleaning example to illustrate my point.

Say I have thirty windows to clean, and I know I can complete the task at *autopilot speed* in forty-five minutes. But if I take a few moments to consciously speed up, I can complete the task in less than thirty minutes. So what do I do? First, I tell myself, "I'm really going to hustle through these thirty windows." Then I concentrate on all the movements, making sure each movement is as efficient as possible. I'm not wasting time by making unnecessary movements. I simply concentrate on working efficiently.

If I charged $45 for that job and completed it in forty-five minutes, that is one dollar per minute of work or $60 an hour. If I consciously speed up and finish the job in less than thirty minutes—for ease of math let's say 22.5 minutes—I've doubled my hourly rate, right? Now take that time saved and multiply it throughout the day. *Just by focusing and speeding up, I've doubled my dollars per hour for the day.* {Sweet Tip} That is one way to maximize profit.

Another way is to simply charge more. This, too, can add up throughout the day or week or year. Instead of charging $45 for the previously mentioned job, let's say I charge $60. If the job still takes me forty-five minutes on autopilot speed, that still leaves me at $75 an hour. If I throw in my focused attention and complete the same job in half the time, my hourly wage just shot up to $150! Now if I add $15 to each job throughout the day and hustle through them, I've just maximized my profit.

These two methods might make the biggest impact when trying to maximize profit, but very simple and small adjustments can make a significant difference, too. Much like with debt and the fact that not one bill/expense is going to bury you, increasing profit is the culmination of many things…maybe you cannot save sixty minutes on one job, but you can save five minutes on twelve jobs. Basic and simple things, like having the right tools for each specific job, can help tremendously. Walking back and forth to your vehicle—or worse, driving back and forth from a job to your home—because you forgot a necessary tool can really dig into your profit margin. Trust me. I don't know how many times one of my employees has left the shop only to return fifteen minutes later because he forgot his tool belt. That's a half hour of lost time. Multiply that by two guys and you have an hour of lost time, which can get expensive quickly. Lucky for you, you'll only have yourself to worry about.

Knowing where you are going ahead of time and not getting lost improves your day's wages, too. If you're involved with a business that includes numerous stops throughout the day, you should lay out a specific route ahead of time. Hopefully your parents will let you borrow their GPS or you have your own. There is no bigger waste of time than to drive from one side of town to the other just to drive back again. Know where your first job will be and plan accordingly.

If you're involved with a service that you provide at your home, the same idea applies. If you have ten accounts to work on for one day and four of those just need a small amount of time each, get those out of the way first. Don't get stuck working on one project for most of the day and then rush through the rest. The typical person loses efficiency as the day goes on. I always seem to get more done in the morning than the afternoon. The start of a project of any sort is usually less efficient than the middle of the project. So starting small projects in the afternoon, when you are less productive, is a bad match. Do the small jobs (more starts) in the morning, when your productivity is highest. Then, when you have a longer project, you can roll with it all afternoon. Maximizing profit will become easier with time, and time is critical to maximizing profit. Use your time wisely and the profits grow. Be organized and the profits grow. Work swiftly and the profits grow.

Hustle but don't hurry

So in order to make more dollars per hour, you need to work faster. How fast can you realistically complete that job? Should you run between windows, hurdle the dog, jump off the top of the ladder so you don't have to climb down? Go crazy-fast and make a lot of money, right?

Not quite. First, let's talk safety. With some jobs there is an element of danger whether it be heights, power equipment, or trip-and-fall hazards. It all depends on what you are doing. You never want to work at an unsafe speed. Second, the finished product never seems to be quite right when you rush through the job. You miss details, and things look sloppy. Third and most important, the customer is watching you work. Many times the customer will be witness to how you work, and the impression that the customer has of you is very important. Does the customer think you are hustling and working hard or rushing to get finished? There's a fine line there.

It's not just your speed that the customer uses to form an impression. If you are incredibly professional, polite, and focused and you move fast, then the customer will think you are hustling. If you showed up late, text half the time, and move fast, he or she will think you are rushing.

With all this talk about speed and moving a little bit faster to increase your dollars per hour, I will advise this: *Never sacrifice quality for speed.* {**Sweet Tip**} Going too fast will increase the likeliness of errors, whether they're in the form of poor workmanship or damages. Work at a speed that is comfortable for you to properly finish the job. Speed comes with time. Once you are proficient at your skill and the more you do it, the faster you will be.

Reducing distractions

Friends, phone calls, Facebook, texting, talking to the neighbor, lunch breaks. The effect of these distractions can be devastating from a dollars per hour perspective. Let's face it: your friends' first priority is not to see that you pay for college. My guess is that not one text of the five hundred you received this week had anything to do with your paying for college. I'm not saying that texting, checking Facebook, or talking on the phone are bad, but doing these things while working will ensure a lower hourly rate. So what if I text a couple times during a job? Let's look at a very real situation. I am cleaning windows and my friend/girlfriend/whoever texts me. I holster my tools, read the text, and respond. This goes on for five minutes. No big deal! So I lost five minutes. Translation: at $50.00 an hour, that is 83 cents a minute. I just reduced my hourly rate to $45.85. If I do that once each hour and work for eight hours, I spent $33.20 on texting. But that's not the only effect. When you stop to text, you are stopping momentum and will need to start up your task again. It's just like starting up your computer. It takes a minute for your brain to process the task at hand, get your tools out, etc.; and starting a task is always slower than if you are rolling with momentum. Now it's not very easy to attach a dollar amount to this, but you see what I am talking about. Just because your friend didn't have anything to do and texted you. *If you text for ten minutes each hour, you have lowered your hourly rate to around $40.* {Sweet Tip}

Momentum

Momentum on a job is real and can be the difference between being very efficient or not efficient at all. Say you have a job painting windows on a house. If you show up to paint one window each day for a week, you will spend a lot of time setting up and breaking down. That's a lot of stirring paint, cleaning the brush out, putting tools away, etc. Whereas if you set up once and paint all day, you are spending more time getting the job done. Say you are cleaning windows on a two-story house that requires twenty-foot ladder work and some stepladder work. Start with the twenty-foot ladder and do all the windows that require it first. Then after all the twenty-foot ladder work is done, do all the stepladder work. This maximizes the momentum of using the same ladder move after move.

Momentum also works in other areas. Say you want to drop five hundred flyers. It will take you less time if you just go out and drop all the flyers in one shot. If you take a few days, then you are wasting the time to get back to that target neighborhood. I have always been known for working long days. Even when I was a teenager, I would work long days. The reason is momentum. I would rather work one fourteen-hour day than two seven-hour days. Why stop when I'm in the rhythm? Just keep going and get more done.

Want to charge like the pros? Then do what the pros do

Make lists. List the things you need to do every day, so you don't forget them. As you get busier, this will become more important. I always kept a yellow legal pad in my car. I know, old school. I could do it on my phone, but then I wouldn't have the satisfaction of crossing things off with my old-school number 2 pencil. I added to the list all day long. Things that needed to be done, people to call, things to pick up, etc. Then at night I would make a new list for the following day, taking everything that didn't get done on today's list and moving it to tomorrow's list. So the next day I would have a nice clean list to work from. Believe me, if you carry your list all day, you will get more done. I still do this exercise to this day.

Keep a schedule. Keep it on your phone, in your computer, in a planner—just keep a schedule of where and when you need to be at certain times. Schedule yourself to call customers back every morning at eight o'clock. Schedule to load your equipment every day at eight-thirty. Schedule jobs, schedule estimates, schedule time off. Scheduling activities will keep you consistent and on task as well as keeping you from forgetting things.

Fill your days with work. If you do not *intentionally* try to fill up your days, you will end up working half days. You have to make filling your schedule a conscious effort. If you are looking at your schedule and you see that Thursday afternoon is free next week, make it a point to find something for that time frame. It will cause you to be more proactive with finding and scheduling work.

Get organized. Wasting time looking for a tool or a misplaced phone number will eat away at your dollars per hour. Keep everything in its place. I would keep my car organized so that I knew where every tool was. I kept all customer information in one place. I would keep my job sites organized. I always put my bucket in the same place (on the front porch) at every job. Organization is a skill that will serve you well for the rest of your life in many, many areas.

Controlling expenses

Another huge way to maximize profit is to minimize expenses. This doesn't mean go cheap on important things like quality work tools, however, because in the end that won't save you money. What you want to watch are the little things, the everyday items you don't give much thought to. After all, everything you spend cuts into the tuition money that's going into the bank. When you buy squeegee rubbers, buy a gross not a dozen. The gross price is better per rubber, and the shipping cost is better since you are ordering a large quantity. Buy your cleaning supplies in bulk at a large-box store, not the gas station. Don't charge things on your credit card unless it's a necessary work purchase, and always pay off the balance at the end of the month to avoid interest charges. Be careful of the daily small purchases.

Feeling rich? Go to the bank. Do not pass Go; go directly to the bank

When you are bringing in $50 per hour, it's real easy to say, "I made a lot of money today, so I can treat myself." Driving home from a good day of work with $400 in your pocket is a dangerous situation. Heck, your friend only made $60 today, so why can't you just spend $100 out on the town tonight? You still made $340 more than your friend made. I call this phenomenon *feeling rich*.

The feeling-rich period is that very short span of time—usually right after you are paid for a job—when you have the money right there in your pocket. And it feels good! A wad of cash that is literally so hot it's burning a hole in your pocket. This is where discipline comes in because that wad of cash also causes poor decision-making. You feel rich right now, but you are not rich! Because you have money in one hand and you don't have your tuition bill in the other hand doesn't mean you are rich. Feeling rich is a high, much like a drug. It can cause you to do stupid things, things you will regret. So what should you do when you are feeling rich? Go to the bank! Go directly to the bank. Do not pass Go. Make your deposit.

Believe me, after you put that money in the bank, that impression of feeling rich will go away; and you will come back to your senses. Having money in your pocket doesn't make you rich; it means you have more money to throw at your ominous tuition bill. There will also be days when you feel broke. You will have to fight with that feeling, too. It's demoralizing when you are working hard and the bills are growing faster than the money you are making. Say you get your tuition bill and you only have half of it in the bank. It's a sick feeling, one that you should remember. Because if you don't get that tuition paid ahead of time, you will have that feeling every month after you graduate when your student loan bill arrives. This is the feeling that we are trying to avoid by having you make as much money as you can now. On those days when you feel broke, you just need to put your head down and get to work because at some point that customer will pay you and you will feel rich again.

Systems

People are generally happier when things go smoothly, whether it's regarding work, relationships, or sports. One way to increase the odds of things going smoothly is to create systems. Systems are a general idea that can benefit almost any aspect of life, but we are just going to deal with work. A good system can increase your efficiency exponentially. Within a couple years, I started utilizing a system for every one of my window cleaning jobs. I had certain ways of doing things, and I replicated those ways at every house. Henry Ford taught us all about that with the assembly line.

For example, when I took out triple-track storm windows, I would take them out the same way and stack them exactly the same way each time. So when I cleaned them and put them back, each window was facing the right direction in the right order. Today I still bid houses with the same system I used when I was eighteen. I start in the front, walk to the right side of the house, and walk around that way counting windows in sections. Because I do it the same way and have done so for so long, I rarely miss anything. I actually have a system for when I talk to customers on the phone, too. I take down all the information on a customer form that I designed with spaces for all the info I need. Name, address, phone number, etc.

Most customers will have the same questions or variations of those same questions. Remember my lines that I practiced? I would use the same answers over and over. By using the same answers with customers, you will be very consistent with information, which is just another system. You may not need to reinvent the wheel when it comes to systems. When you train, watch for the systems your employer uses. Professionals in any trade figure out rather quickly that systems will increase efficiency. *Systems maximize profits.* [**Sweet Tip**]

You don't need your buddy's help

It never fails. Your friends will find out that you are making several times what they are making in their summer jobs, and they will want in on the action. A friend will want to *help you* on a job for $15 an hour or some crazy high number your friend comes up with. To him it makes sense. But to you it doesn't. In fact, it's dangerous in several ways. First, that friend will not have the skills you have. After all, you trained and learned and you are furthering your knowledge of the trade by self-educating. You can't rely on someone who doesn't have the training you have. Your buddy will inevitably screw up your job, too; it's just a matter of when. Your buddy may not have the manners or customer service skills you do either. Looking bad in front of the customer will reflect negatively on you, not him. That is a risk you cannot afford. And speaking of expensive risks, if he gets hurt on the job you will be looking at much bigger problems than just his screwing up a job. Finally, and most importantly, why share the profit? You worked very hard marketing and selling so keep all the profits!

Acceptable low-paying jobs

With all this talk of $50 per hour and maximizing your profits, let's not be unrealistic when it comes to times when there are no opportunities or the work you normally do for higher profit is out of season. Maybe you have a heavy class load or some classes that require a lot of labs, yet you still need some cash flow. Maybe you can only find low-paying jobs during the hours you can work. Sometimes you just have to take what's available. Here are a couple things to look for.

If you can find a job where you can study while you work, you are golden. Study while working? Am I crazy? There are jobs that allow for that. Some security jobs will let you read while you sit and wait for the next visitor to sign in. Babysitting is another perfect example. The kids are in bed and it's study time! I think we have all seen the college student studying behind the counter of a convenience store. Now I am not saying to study when you are supposed to be working. What I am saying is, if the job allows for studying, then that is advantageous. After all, you are attending college so you will need to study. You might as well get paid for it.

Another thing to look for when you need to take a lower-paying job is the possibility of jobs where tips are involved. Waiters, waitresses, and bartenders usually get paid a wage plus tips. Ah, tips. We all know that older folks and college students are the worst tippers, right? Not necessarily. Almost always, the tips you do receive have everything to do with how well you took care of the customer. If you never refilled the drinks, forgot part of the order, or were rude, expect little or no tip. If you provided exceptional service, expect that normal 15 to 20 % gratuity. What I like about working for tips is that *you* can have an effect on the tip amount. Another good thing about the waiting tables/bartending-type jobs is that there are usually night hours available. Since most classes are during the day, you can pick up work hours at night.

Mentors

I had a customer in Rochester named Jack Genthner. I call him a customer, but he was more of a mentor. He was a retired gentleman, who always wanted to talk business with me. He had owned his own business, and he liked the idea of a high school student working for himself. The Kid Card in its finest form. He always used to say, "Remember your customers now; you will need those experiences later." Thinking back now I realize this is amazingly true because, with every customer interaction, you learn something, especially those first customers. Jack Genthner was mentoring me and I didn't even know it. He took the time to teach me business skills.

Jack Genthner also had a 32' ladder, and my tallest ladder was 20.' He would let me borrow his when I needed it. I only needed it a couple times, but I couldn't have completed those jobs without it. I didn't want to buy one for just a couple jobs, so I just borrowed Jack's. I cleaned a few extra windows for Jack in return for borrowing the ladder, but I think he was just happy to help me out. Jack was a guy who was willing to give a hardworking kid an opportunity, and I seized that opportunity. Jack is deceased now, but I will always remember his advice and support in my early business ventures. If you are fortunate enough to find a mentor or two, open your ears and listen. That advice might be some of the best advice you ever get because a good mentor will have your best interest at heart.

Self-educating

Regardless of what service you provide, there is always more you can learn. It is mind-numbing how much information is out there when it comes to cleaning windows. There are magazines, websites, online forums and videos, professional organizations, seminars, and the list goes on. To this day I still self-educate almost every day. I very much prefer to be the expert who is on top of all things window cleaning. Things change and people come up with great new ideas to solve old problems. Self-educating is a way to be that expert. It's the way to become that go-to guy we mentioned earlier. Say you spend a half hour each day researching online. After one year you are 180 hours more knowledgeable than the next guy. *Problems come from lack of knowledge, and profits are made by those with the most knowledge.* {**Sweet Tip**}

Be the best by knowing the most. Keep studying because, once you educate yourself, you can educate the customer; and educating the customer will do wonders for your credibility.

Intangibles count

Spirit, attitude, confidence, creativity, discipline, and business savvy are all intangibles that come from within. Yet they shine through to everyone you meet. Maybe you have these qualities now; maybe you will get them later. Either way begin recognizing them and start improving the ones that need it.

Throughout this whole program we talk about the Kid Card, which exemplifies these qualities. These intangibles seep into everything you do, whether at work or in your personal life. If a high school student is confident and has a good attitude, success is more likely. If a student has a bad attitude, success is unlikely. It really is easy to excel working for yourself if you can tap into these qualities. You are the person making all the decisions and doing all the work. Be proud of what you are doing because it is admirable. Paying for college is no small deal. It's huge. And not everyone can do it. Harness those intangibles, build your lemonade stand, play the Kid Card, serve the best damn lemonade in town, and you will be the 10. Graduating debt-free is as easy as that.

CHAPTER 8

For the parents:
Smile, you may not have to pay for your kid's college education

We all want our children to succeed. I certainly do. And there are thousands of parenting books explaining what success really means. However, there is one book that addresses paying for college and avoiding debt through hard work—and you are holding it. Your kid came home with this book called *Lemonade Stand Economics*. The book says that if you work hard enough and smart enough starting in high school, you can pay for college working for yourself and graduate with no debt. Sound too good to be true? It's not. It's absolutely possible, and I know students who are doing it right now.

In today's economy a college education is a decided advantage. That college degree is an admirable goal for any high school student. My sons don't know anything different. They just know they are going to college after high school. But there is a hurdle, and it's a big one. This hurdle can seem a hundred feet tall. In fact, it can seem so high that most people choose to run under it to avoid it. That hurdle is the cost of college. College is expensive. Not just the tuition, but there are room and board, books, transportation, the cell phone, and the list goes on. Increasingly, high school students are picking among colleges that cost the least instead of going to the college they want to attend or the school that provides the best education for their field of study.

What happened to attending college for a specific program? Or going to the best school your grades will get you into? What happened to maximizing your potential? Often it's the money. Some students simply can't afford the college they want to attend. The scenario where parents pay for their child's college education is becoming less common, forcing these students to pay for it themselves. That's where I was when I graduated from high school. I applied to college knowing that I had to pay every dime.

Paying for college is stressful for parents and their children. Being a parent is hard; being college-bound is, too. Take an eighteen-year-old high school student who worked hard for four years to graduate with good grades, got into the college he wanted to attend, and now is looking at paying $50,000 or $90,000 or $150,000 for that college degree. Paying for college is highly stressful for anyone who doesn't already have the money sitting in the bank (and those situations are becoming more and more rare). This stress is not solely placed on the student. Parents are cashing in 401(k)s and taking out second mortgages to pay for college. That eighteen-year-old may have held part time jobs in high school, but her part-time jobs aren't going to touch that tuition bill. So what is a student to do? Is there any help? Right now the most realistic option, what seems like the only option, is to take out student loans. There are scholarships and grants available, but the majority of the money for college costs is still coming from student loans. More than $100 billion in federal education loans are originated each year. So we're saying that the only real option is debt? This is how we treat the next generation? Really? Because debt as the only option sucks! It's just wrong. Let me throw some horribly sour stats at you.

 According to the NCES, 66 % of college freshmen reported having grave concerns about being able to finance their education.

 Two thirds of college seniors graduated with loans in 2011, and they carried an average of $26,600 in debt. In the coming years, many of these graduates will still be paying off their student loans when it's time for their kids to go to college.

 New graduates often taste this new reality; their first loan payments come due within sixty days after graduation. The Class of 2011 also faced the highest unemployment rate for young college graduates in recent history at 9.1%.

According to the Department of Education, only 54% of students graduate within six years. (This means that 46% do not graduate.)

 According to the NCES, by eleventh and twelfth grades more than 90% of students reported having discussions about academic requirements or the type of college to attend. However, less than 50% reported discussing college costs or financial aid.

 In the last two decades, the cost of public four-year colleges more than tripled. During that same time, the cost of private four-year and public two-year colleges more than doubled.

 As of October 2011, total outstanding student debt has passed $1 trillion, more than the nation's credit card debt.

The fact that the only *real* option high school graduates in America have to pay for college is by amassing debt is a failure on all our parts. The banks (backed by our government) are helping struggling students by placing them into a whirlpool of debt to attain a higher education. A college degree is a big investment, probably one of the most important investments a person can make. There's no doubt that a college degree is worth the price, but the culture we have created due to high college costs and the easily attained student loans results in massive personal debt upon graduation. Is this what you really want for your child? Work hard studying for four years to walk across the stage with your mortar board on as the head of your department hands you a well-deserved diploma...and a bill. A huge bill. You owe thousands of dollars. No, tens of thousands or in some cases more than $100,000. Congratulations, you have a college degree and you are buried in debt. Debt that will plague you for decades. So, realistically, what can we do to change that scenario? Is there another option? Yes, there is and you are holding the playbook in your hands.

Lemonade Stand Economics - A refreshing way to pay for college

I wrote this book to give ambitious college-bound students another option to pay for college. It frustrates me to hear that students are compromising their choice of colleges because of cost. It makes me sick to know that most college graduates are starting off their adult life with high levels of unnecessary debt. High school students, or college students for that matter, have never really felt the pain of debt. They simply don't know what they are getting into when they sign those student loan documents. As parents you likely have felt the pain of debt. You may still be paying your own student loans as your child signs for his or hers. The good news is it doesn't have to be that way.

It's funny how, as you get older and your own children grow, you start to think back to the experiences that shaped who and where you are today. Some of these experiences make you proud, and some do not. There are things you wouldn't change and others you wish you'd done just a little differently. I think back to how I paid for college. Call it being oblivious, but all I knew was that I was going to college and I was working to pay for it. However, I was not doing what most teens were doing for a summer job. I did it differently. I was working for myself cleaning windows. And I wasn't working for minimum wage either—or even double that paltry sum. I was earning more than ten times minimum wage at that time.

Looking back I realize that what I did was admirable, but it wasn't unique. Any teenager with a good idea, ambition, and a good work ethic can do it, too. The problem lies in the fact that most teenagers have no clue that they are capable of working for themselves. And if they are aware of their capabilities, they probably don't know where to start. This is where *Lemonade Stand Economics* comes in.

If a hardworking teenager did what I did in high school in terms of making money—and had just a bit of guidance with financial planning—graduating from college debt-free would be totally realistic. I did make a lot of money in my teen years, but I also spent foolishly. Then I graduated from college with $15,000 in student loans because I didn't know any better. I was never taught about spending and saving, time management, or the pain of debt. I was presented with all kinds of *free money* in the form of student loans. Not one person ever told me, "Hey, wait! Don't take the student loan!" I had the capacity to pay for school without taking out student loans, but I didn't. Lured by low interest rates and long payoff periods, I bit... hook, line and sinker. Maybe this happened to you too. Please don't let this happen to your child! Even if you don't help him or her do everything as it's laid out in this book, at least have a conversation (or a dozen!) about money, finances, debt, and your kid's future.

Lemonade Stand Economics offers a real life solution. I've outlined a strategy with one goal: debt-free college graduation from working for yourself. That is the means to the end of breaking that student loan debt cycle. We are not creating the next Fortune 500 corporation here. This isn't about creating an empire; it's about paying for college. I am not telling students to choose now what they'll do for the rest of their lives. I am just looking to guide your son or daughter through a better way to pay for college as well as helping him or her learn valuable business and life skills that are simply not taught in high school. This program can save your child from debt and teach this teenager about life, business, and him- or herself along the way.

I urge you to read the first seven chapters of the book in order to fully understand what your child will learn by deciding to dive in and enter the world of working for him- or herself. This is not a multilevel marketing scheme. It's not one of those empty-promises, *you-can-do-it* speeches. This is different. This is about high school students investing in themselves, where they are their own products and their talents are their inventory. This program is for someone looking to pay for college and make a difference in the world.

Lemonade Stand Economics will show your high school student how to make two, three, and four times what his or her friends make slapping sandwiches together. The book offers realistic guidance as to where to start and how to work for yourself. But it's not just about earning money. This program includes many facets of small business that, once learned, will carry over into future careers. I would even go so far as to say that the educational aspect of the program is actually more important long-term than the money-making aspect. There is advice on how to market, advertise, and find customers. The book covers simple concepts like how to meet, greet, and shake hands with customers. It also covers complicated concepts like bidding jobs, estimating the amount of time involved, and asking for referrals. And don't forget the most important concept when you work for yourself: how to serve up a steamin' hot plate of fantastic customer service.

From day one through year four, there is realistic advice specifically for teenagers to help them maximize their potential and their earnings. All with the goal of putting money into their pockets to pay for college now instead of paying student loan payments later. This program is primarily focused toward working during summer breaks and weekends, utilizing time and money management so it will not hurt students' grades.

This is a program with multiple steps. As an adult you already know that success doesn't happen overnight and there are no shortcuts. This program includes training, learning, and a lot of work. But like most things, as time goes by it gets easier, and eventually your teenager will start seeing the dollars earned per hour increase, and the goal of paying for college will get much closer. I've done this program, and so have others. I learned to clean windows when I was sixteen, working as summer help. If I had stayed cleaning windows as an employee when I was seventeen, I would've kept making $3.35 an hour.

But instead I took my skills in a different direction and started making $20 per hour, then the next year $40, and after that $50. I tell my readers if they are going to work for an hour make, sure they are compensated handsomely for it. I was cleaning windows, the same task I did working for someone else and taking the same amount of time to do it. After that first summer, however, I did it differently and purposefully and for myself. The result was that I made significantly more money per hour, learned a lot about business, and had a sense of pride in doing it.

Maybe only parts of the program will work for your teenager, so he or she ends up making $20 an hour and graduates from college with $5,000 in debt instead of $15,000. The life and business lessons are still there, and less debt is better than more. Maybe your kid, after reading the book, ends up only making double what he or she would make slapping sandwiches together. That is awesome! Think about that in terms of your own job. If you could do your same job, just in a different way, and give yourself a 100 % pay raise, that might be a life-changer. Your teenager's skill doesn't have to be cleaning windows. For some people just the thought of climbing a ladder is enough to make them break out in a sweat. Rest assured that there are numerous ways to make above-average earnings, many of which are listed in the book. In fact, in writing this book, I found several students who are earning above-average wages and in many different ways. The possibilities are endless.

Parental support

At this point if you still think this program can't possibly work or it's a waste of time, then you are dismissed. You may now stop reading, turn on the nightly news or the latest reality show, and tune out. Nothing great was ever accomplished without enthusiasm. If you are not enthusiastic about this, then I beg of you not to stifle your teenager's enthusiasm. Do not discourage your child from this endeavor or say that it won't work. Several people told me I couldn't do it when I was a teenager, and I proved them all wrong. Be as supportive as you can; and if you can't be supportive, then kindly stay out of your kid's way. Once you're finished with this chapter, I strongly encourage you again to start reading from the beginning to get a complete overview of what the program entails. By doing so, not only will this chapter make more sense, but you will know what your teenager is talking about. Reading through the book together may even spark more ideas than those I've presented.

For me one of the most exciting times as a parent is when my child does something fantastic. You know what I'm talking about. You didn't ask him to do it. He did it on his own in his own way, and he did it well. Whether the *it* is picking up the living room without being asked, starring in the school musical, or catching a football one-handed to win the game, we've all experienced these moments with our kids. Think of how you will feel when your son or daughter graduates from college having paid for it with no parental help and no debt. That is such an outstanding accomplishment, almost beyond words.

There are basic characteristics we all wish for our children to have: confidence, motivation, intelligence, work ethic, discipline. Now maybe your son or daughter currently possesses only a few of these characteristics. Could this program bring out the others? I'd venture to say yes. I discuss the motivation spectrum in chapter 3. (Also, see the graphic below.) Everyone is somewhere on the motivation spectrum. A 1 is a lazy couch dweller, and a 10 is a motivated overachiever. Maybe your kid is a 4. Could you as a parent help your child rise to a 6 or 7 level? What if your kid is an 8? Can you help guide him or her to being a 10? Your role may not be what you think it will be.

Motivation Spectrum

Some teens will take on only a part of this program, and that's OK. Maybe your teen doesn't complete the entire program and ends up working as an employee for most of these upcoming years. But maybe she picks up side jobs along the way for $15 an hour. I call that a success! Maybe your teen takes the initial steps and then realizes working for himself is just not his style, but he really liked designing the flyers. In this case he could find a graphic design job. For most any aspect of this program, after attempting to complete a section, the teenager who attempts but fails will still be more enriched than before she tried it.

Simply due to lack of exposure, people in this age group don't necessarily know what type of work they like. These are the years of exploration; this is the time for trial and error and experimentation. This book gives some entrepreneurial guidance in an arena that just isn't presented in school. And if you think your child can't do it, well, maybe you'll be surprised when she does.

So how can you help?

Remember that day way back when...even though it seems like yesterday... when you were a lot younger and your child was five years old and wearing that first bike helmet. The day you took the training wheels off. You ran behind that bike, holding it steady as your youngster pedaled. The next thing you knew, you were just standing there in the street as your child pedaled away, all wobbly but still upright. There was that first fall, followed by a couple tears. So you gave your best mini-motivational speech about how well she did and that she should try again. Then again, you ran behind the bike holding the seat, but this time you had to run a little faster and not nearly as long before you were standing alone again watching her pedal away. This time she was less wobbly and not looking back. You didn't make the bike move or power it; you just kept it steady and going in the right direction until your child was able to handle it on her own. She only needed your help those first couple tries. Then after a while, she got the hang of it and there was no need for dear old Mom's or Dad's help anymore.

This is how I see the parents' role with *Lemonade Stand Economics*. Starting is the hardest part. Just like riding a bike, getting that bike moving the first time is challenging. Then, after your child pedals around the block a few times, it gets easier. The next thing you know, she is biking all over the neighborhood. Believe it or not, working for yourself as a teenager can be like that, too...before you know it, it's like she or he is riding a bike.

I am a parent of two young boys, and I understand parental concerns. The best interest of our children is always priority one. What do you do when things go wrong? How should you as the parent react? Maybe your kid tries and fails, which can happen. Or will he make it look easy? Some children may ask or expect their parents to do too much. I mean, it's not the parents' job to drive them around, double-check their schedules, and talk to irate customers who might call when things go wrong.

The way I see it, anyone can learn these life lessons now as a teenager or later in the first job out of college. Our role as parents is important. First we help our children learn to walk and talk, then read and write. Then the next day they are driving and graduating from high school. When your child is a teenager, parenting isn't as glamorous or fun as when he or she was learning to walk and looked to you for everything. But the guidance you do or don't provide at this impressionable age will affect his or her life forever.

I want to help my sons embrace who they are and realize what they can do. I want to be involved but not too involved. I want to guide them but not do it for them. Does the parenting ever stop? As a parent you know the answer to that question. I will say this: if you can't be involved or don't believe in it, at least don't be an enthusiasm vacuum. This adventure is a big deal. It's a lot of fun, a lot of work, and potentially life-changing.

Examples of how you can help as a parent

Support/encouragement. Confidence is a huge part of success. Being there to celebrate successes as well as listening when things don't go right is very beneficial to anyone's confidence level. Support but don't coddle; listen and advise just enough to help your teenager make the right decision on her own. Encourage her when she's ready to give up and help her focus when she becomes distracted.

Marketing. Refer your friends. Hang some flyers at work. My mother did both for me as well as printing all my flyers. This is an invaluable help that can free up time for your teen, which is already scarce. You may be the one to get the ball rolling for your child's venture.

The car. If your teen doesn't have a car, let him use your car to get around. Maybe make a deal that, for the use of the car, he will at the very least wash and vacuum it every weekend.

Planning/budgeting. Much to the dismay of the average teen, adults do know more than he or she does! Assistance when it comes to budgeting, planning, and organizing can be very beneficial coming from a supportive parent. You can help keep the planning realistic and your child's eye on the prize.

Finding opportunities. You may see opportunities right in front of your child's eyes that he or she may not. You may be able to create opportunities through your work, business associates, organizations, and friends. This, too, might provide the initial spark. Success breeds success; it creates momentum. Look for and offer up the opportunities you see.

Motivation. Would it surprise you if I said that some teens have trouble getting up and getting to work in the morning? That's what I thought! Some high schoolers need a little assistance in the motivation department. Nudge but don't push; after all, this is *her* program, not yours. Maybe as a gift you can buy your teen one of the old-fashioned bell alarm clocks. Get a real loud one too, that will really wake her up!

Accountability. As adults we are used to having a sense of accountability. This concept may be new to a teenager working for himself. That teen may not understand the importance. Explain to him the difference between being a teenager and high school student and being a teenager working for himself. He can't ditch out on jobs because his friends are going to the beach. That's not the way it works.

Being polite and professional. Hopefully your child is already polite. Being professional may need some work. I do address this topic at length, but some good-old practice shaking hands with Dad isn't going to hurt.

Finding that first training job. Finding a job in the trade or skill your teen wants to learn isn't always easy. Sometimes dear old Mom can help with that job. Or, even better, she may know someone in the business. One approach you might want to use is being honest about what your child is attempting. If *you* explain the situation to the prospective employer, the employer might be impressed enough to hire your teen on, as opposed to your teen making wild claims about his or her aspirations.

Talk to your kid about money. And listen to what she says, too. She may not have all that much experience dealing with money. Getting $50 for your birthday is different than receiving a check from a customer. Money management is a key element throughout the book, and having a parent with one eye on the bank balance isn't going to hurt.

FROM THE AUTHOR

I want to see my boys go to the colleges of their choice…regardless of the cost. I don't want to see my kids (or anyone else's for that matter) start their adult life in debt. I sincerely hope that this program changes the lives of many college-bound students. I'm not just talking about financially either. It wasn't until I wrote this book that I realized the most important aspect of my working for myself as a teenager was not the money but the education in small business that I received. By working for myself, I learned a whole toolbox of skills that I carried with me into future professions. Skills like time management, money management, customer service, scheduling, expense management, selling, bidding, marketing, and advertising. These are all skills a person needs to learn at some point, so why shouldn't your teen learn them now and make some serious money doing it? It's like the ideal real-life internship. Instead of paying for his or her education, your teen is getting paid for an education.

If your teenager can learn the concept of earning more than he or she spends, the result will be growing up to be financially free to invest in the future and maximize the power of his or her income. Debt robs a person of that ability. Working for yourself is an exciting adventure—hard work and growing up included. The maturity gained and knowledge learned firsthand trump the financial results, although owing zero dollars upon college graduation comes in a close second. I'm excited for your college-bound teen, and I hope you are even more excited. My goal with this book is that, in a few years, at least one reader shoots me an e-mail or Facebook message that says, "I paid for college, graduated debt-free, and learned valuable business skills because of Lemonade Stand Economics."

Thanks for reading. Now go back to the beginning, get your brainstorming engines started, and help your teen take off on this life-changing journey!

APPENDIX

The Gameplan Worksheet

The Gameplan is specifically designed to help you with goal-setting as you lay out the financial aspects of working for yourself. Note that you will need to fill this out before summer starts each year because costs and timeframes change from year to year.

Section 1: Financial goals   **College costs**

College you plan on attending: _____

Cost of 4 years at that college: _____
(if you don't know, use the national average of $88,000) ex. $88,000

Add 10%   +_____
                                                  ex. $8,800

Total cost of 4 years at college   =_____
                                                  ex. $96,800

Depending on when you start , you may have several summers to pay for that first year of college, so let's focus on that.

First-year cost   _____
equation: (total cost above/4)   *ex. $24,200 = ($96,800/4)*
Scholarships   −_____
                                 ex. $1,000

Grants   −_____
ex. Pell grant   *ex. $700*

Other (help from parents, etc.)   −_____
ex. Parents saved for college   *ex. $1,500*

Total cost of first year in college   =_____
                                 ex. $21,000

Therefore your college savings goal while you are in high school will be $21,000.

Savings goal: First year of college

Number of summers before you start college?   _____
                              ex. 2 (if you start after junior year)

Savings goal per summer   _____
equation: (Cost of first year/no. of summers before college) ex. $10,500

Option 1: Working summers only
Daily savings goal: _____
equation: (summer savings goal / 60 work days)   *ex. $175*

Target $ / hour to accomplish this daily goal   _____
equation: (daily savings goal / 8 hours)   *ex. $21.87*

Can you meet the daily goal in the summer?   Yes?   No?
If No, go to option 2   *(circle one)*

Option 2: Working summers and one weekend a month
Daily savings goal   _____
equation: (summer/weekend savings goal / 84 work days) ex. $125

Target $ / hour to accomplish this daily goal   _____
equation: (daily savings goal / 8hrs)   *ex. $15.63*

- All of the equations above are based on the following, which may or may not be correct for your situation.
- We are assuming you work 5 days a week in the summer (approximately 60 days).
- We are assuming a work day is 8 hours. The examples assume you are a high school junior. If you are a sophomore or senior, the example answers would be different.

Section 2: Jobs

Now that you know how much you will need to save, you can figure out what job interests you enough to accomplish those savings goals.

Jobs you would like to do:	Jobs you don't want to do:
Add anything you wouldn't mind doing.	
_____	_____
_____	_____
_____	_____
_____	_____
_____	_____
_____	_____
_____	_____
_____	_____
_____	_____

Now rank the jobs you would like to do first to last, and do some research on your top three. What did you learn from your research?

1. _____

2. _____

3. _____

4. _____

Who will you contact about training jobs?

1. _____

2. _____

3. _____

Section 3: Starting to work for yourself

At this point you have trained and have experience and knowledge in your skill. You have started doing side jobs, and you are ready to start on your own.

Before you start, answer the following questions.

Are you still interested in this job?   Yes   No
Will it pay well enough to accomplish your goals?   Yes   No

If Yes, great! If No, then lets readdress your job choice. It's better to know now than later if something doesn't fit.

Start-up costs:

List what you will need to start:
ex. Business cards, signs, tools, equipment, supplies, marketing materials, etc.

Item	Cost
_____	_____
_____	_____
_____	_____
_____	_____
_____	_____
_____	_____
_____	_____
_____	_____
_____	_____
	Total: _____

Start-up expense average daily cost:　　　　$_____

equation: (total cost / 60 work days)

Start-up expense average hourly cost:　　　$_____

equation: (daily cost / 8 hours)

Operating expenses:

Operating expenses are items that will need to be replenished over time.
List the total of what you will need for the current year:

ex. Gas, squeegee rubbers, cleaning chemicals, etc.

Item	Cost
_____	_____
_____	_____
_____	_____
_____	_____
_____	_____
_____	_____
_____	_____
_____	_____
_____	_____
_____	_____
	Total: _____

Operating exp. average daily cost: $_____

equation: (total oper. exp. cost / 60 work days)

Operating exp. average hourly cost: $_____

equation: (daily oper. exp. cost / 8 hours)

Total daily costs: $_____

equation: (daily start-up cost + daily oper. exp. cost)

Total hourly costs: $_____

equation: (total daily cost / 8 hours)

This hourly cost can now be applied to your pricing. The key is to keep the costs low so that you can keep or save more of what you earn. Take what you earn per hour and subtract the cost. The result is the amount you will save for college as well as any spending money.

Section 4: When you go to the bank

You will split your money three ways when you go to the bank. Let's figure out what percentage goes where.

Operating expenses account:

You cannot work for yourself without the necessary items that enable you to perform your service. It is the first priority when it comes to depositing money at the bank.

How much do you earn per hour? $_____

How much are your total costs per hour? $_____

% to put into operating expenses account: _____%

equation:
total hourly costs /
dollars per hour earned x 100 = operating expenses %

Spending money account:

Let's be realistic. Everyone needs a little spending money. Be careful with this one. If you deposit too much into this account, you will short the other two accounts.

How much do you earn per hour? $_____

How much spending cash do you *need* in a week? $_____

ex. Food, gas, entertainment

% to put into spending account: _____%

equation:
spending cash needed weekly / 40 /
(dollars per hour earned) x 10 = spending expense %

College savings account:

How much do you earn per hour? $_____
How much are your total costs per hour? $_____

% to put into your college savings account: _____%

equation:
target dollars per hour (from section 1) /
dollars per hour earned x 10 = college savings %)

Add the three percentages going to the bank _____%

equation:
operating expenses % + spending
money % + college savings %

If you are under 100%, take the difference and add it to your college savings %.

If you are over 100%, you need to make cuts in expenses to get your budget to balance. This is a very real scenario for households and businesses. It's not easy, but it's real.

If you find this form confusing, the Gameplan is on the website and the computer can do the math for you. It's more important that you understand the concepts than the math.